I0045689

What we can learn from the Bible about office politics

Dr Michael Teng

Published in 2011 by

Corporate Turnaround Centre Pte Ltd.

Printed in Singapore
by Markono Print Media Pte Ltd

9 8 7 6 5 4 3 2 1
011 012

Copyright © 2011 by Corporate Turnaround Centre Pte Ltd. All rights reserved. This publication is protected by Copyright and permission should be obtained from the publisher prior to any prohibited reproduction, storage in a retrieval system, or transmission in any form or by any means, electronic, mechanical, photocopying, recording, or likewise. For information regarding permission(s), write to: admin@corporateturnaroundcentre.com

Background of Dr Mike Teng

Dr Mike Teng is the author of a best-selling book "Corporate Turnaround: Nursing a sick company back to health", in 2002 which is also translated into the Bahasa Indonesia and Mandarin. His book is endorsed by marketing guru Professor Philip Kotler and business tycoons Mr Oei Hong Leong and Dr YY Wong. He subsequently authored more than twenty two management books on corporate transformation, merger and acquisitions, marketing and general management. Sixteen of them are translated into Mandarin. He is also an author of two Christian books, namely Corporate Wellness: Spiritual and Secular Principles in Corporate Turnaround and Transformation and Jesus: The Corporate Turnaround Expert.

Dr Teng is currently the Managing Director of Corporate Turnaround Centre Pte Ltd (www.corporateturnaroundcentre.com) , founded in 2004 which provides corporate training and investment/management advisory services in the region. He also advised several boards of directors of publicly-listed companies. He has more than 30 years of experience in strategic planning, operational and project management and responsibilities in the Asia Pacific region. Of these, he held Chief Executive Officer's positions for 19 years in multi-national and publicly listed companies.

Dr Teng is the current Senate Member and served as the Executive Council member for fourteen years and the last four years as the President of the Marketing Institute of Singapore (2000 – 2004), the national marketing association. Dr Teng is the President of the National University of Singapore MBA Alumni as well as the President of the University of South Australia alumni and director of the NUS BSA Alumni. He was the President of the Lion City

Toastmaster Club in 1988.

Dr Teng holds a Doctor in Business Administration (DBA) from the University of South Australia, Master in Business Administration (MBA) and Bachelor in Mechanical Engineering (BEng) from the National University of Singapore. He is also a Professional Engineer (P Eng, Singapore), Chartered Engineer (C Eng, UK) and Fellow Member of several prestigious professional institutes namely, Chartered Institute of Marketing (FCIM), Chartered Management Institute (FCMI), Institute of Mechanical Engineers (FIMechE), Marketing Institute of Singapore (FMIS), Institute of Electrical Engineers (FIEE) and Senior Member of Singapore Computer Society (SMSCS). He is also a Practising Management Consultant (PMC) certified by the Singapore government.

OFFICE POLITICS

Table of Contents

INTRODUCTION (1)

The economy gurus have spoken. The economists are of differing opinions even amongst themselves. Whom should we trust when it comes to the current status of the world economy? Will the big guys" actions have any impact on the 'small fries"?

Although there have been many business reports on the welfare of the world economy, you cannot necessarily rely upon in order to predict the future of your job stability. As is known, businesses cannot be sustained without revenue growth; recession-like conditions seem to be sticking around longer than we'd like.

In a recession where jobs are cut more quickly than they develop, then the employment picture would not be heading to any type of recovery until businesses begin substantial investment. How would all these translate to the daily lives of ordinary men and women who are just trying to make a living?

It seems like the harsh world out there has just crept into the office, creating what we know today as the concrete jungle, as world economy has shaken many businesses to where downsizing is justifiable. And the ordinary working men and women are certainly disturbed enough to get on the latest fitness program - survival of the fittest, that is. And that might mean… politics of a different kind. This is the other factor at play that is "recession-proof" – office politics!

OFFICE POLITICS (2)

a. Definition

If you are holding a job right now, even as you are reading this, do your thoughts flit quickly to the question, "for how long?" Perhaps your boss or the Human Resource Department has been reminding you that "no one is indispensable" or that the frequent "budget cut" calls are necessary to keep the business afloat. Thus, a Pandora's Box is opened for some practices which many of us simple working folk would like to avoid. The heavyweight term here is "Office Politics."

This is simply where one worker employs some manipulative mechanism to reaffirm or establish his or her position in the company, even at the expense of others. Sad to say that even without the shaky economic status, this practice has made its way into the office environment in subtle or direct form. Where there are people with personal agendas or when one feels threatened in his or her career, office politics thrives. What happens to the frequency of this existing issue when the economic status is worrisome!

Office politics is a pervasive term; it exists very subtly at the workplace, catching ignorant employees many times unaware. It can even draw one into its web without consent. It is bound to happen when there are differences of personalities and opinions at the workplace.

b. Good and bad politicking

Some experts claim that office politicking is actually healthy to the organization or that, there is good and bad office politicking. Good politicking refers to some practices engaged by the employees or management to secure the good of the employee(s) and the organization. Good politicking is where one exercises good work ethics such as honesty, openness and thoughtful consideration to others at the workplace through clear and objective communication with all involved parties without going behind their backs on any issue or circumstance. Respect and trust are exercised without betraying confidence. Although one may not like what is heard, the truth can be conveyed properly for one to accept graciously for the common good of the organization.

Bad politicking refers to possible damage to the reputation of the organization with some employees succeeding at the expense of other employees. Many unethical practices are prevalent with conflicts arising to the detriment of the company and employees. There are posers and those with bad attitudes who slow down or halt the productivity of the organization. Distrust and manipulation abound at the workplace and no one feels safe while at work.

c. Who needs to know?

If you are working, whether holding a job or running a business, YOU need to know about office politics. Unless you are the sole employee or employer, office politics is sure to surface at some point in the course of your business. Offices have been subtly, or otherwise, turned into power struggle battlegrounds without anyone being the wiser. Suddenly, you are shown the door, clueless of what hit you. Whether you are a newbie or a "wannabe" or a veteran, office politics is no respecter of persons. Whether you are a male or female, office politics invites all to its web circle.

d. Who are involved?

It is noted that women tend to engage in political tactics at the office even though they will feel the impact more when they are the "victims." Hence, there is a double standard for women unless they are wise and alert to the occasion. A woman may unknowingly be engaged in office politics for some reason or another, which might be easily misconstrued by onlookers.

Employees as well as employers may be drawn into this web knowingly or unwittingly. Once they are involved, it takes effort and wisdom to strategize your ascent or exit. Experts have claimed that there is no business, which can be devoid of office politics, and strangely enough, it grows as the business grows. Thus, it is most probable that all levels of employment in a business will be confronted, and engaged with some extent of office politics. How would one handle it? Take the bull by its horns, or shy away from the situation?

But office politicking is not biased toward any gender; it welcomes all to its web of wits. It takes great effort to remove oneself from the entanglement.

e. Survivors and Victims

Office politics has a way of permeating through the walls and space in the office. As the saying goes, "the walls have ears". But nowadays with modern technology, you can get into the "game" easily enough (whether you like it or not), with just an email or a phone call.

As with wars, there are always survivors and casualties, maybe even deaths. Which category you find yourself in depends upon your alertness to, and your strategies in, being on top of office politics. Without a doubt, everyone wants to be a survivor – and you *can* survive at office politics. It is a matter of understanding yourself and others, and putting good practices at the workplace into position to benefit not only yourself and your colleagues, but also the organization you work for, as a whole.

Thus, experts advise that one should be alert to, and be actively engaged in, office politics to ensure your survival in the concrete jungle, created by your own kind.

f. Types of office politics

Office politics can come in many forms and methods. One needs to be skilled in identifying them in order to be aware of their sting and vibes to avoid potential danger and harm to self and others, as well as the company.

The most common form of office politics comes through gossiping. While many may dismiss this activity as harmless or "a fact of life," its consequence is sharper than its sting. You may have also experienced blatant unfairness at the workplace, especially when you are directly affected by the practice; in other words, you do not enjoy the benefits of being part of the clique. There is the solidarity of power through group support when you "belong" to cliques formed in the workplace, or what we call "camps;" this form of office politics is also called networking.

One can also withhold useful information from competitors or rivals in office politicking known as the"no invitation" trick. Other forms of office politics are the creative magpie approach where one takes the credit for another's success. Unethical practices can also cut short your patience, especially when your hands are tied. Being a bystander is when one chooses not to get involved even though the alleged party requires some help or support. Then you have "emailing the gods" or keeping everyone at management level in the loop of your emails to "keep them informed" of your good intentions. Office politicking can also be in the form of making promises through your eloquence for favors or goods desired at the moment; this is known as "jam tomorrow." You may promise the sky but making good on your promises has yet to be seen. It would take a skilled and mature authority to see through these types of foundationless schemes.

Office politics can happen when conflicts between employees or departments arise and where competition within the company is stiff. This can push likeminded employees to collaborate and network for their own benefits without any consideration of others or even the company itself. Selfishness, manipulation, using the trump card, scratching each other's back, hypocrisy and back-stabbing are various forms of office politicking that one should be alert to. People's behavior can also lend fuel to office politics although many practice subtlety and decency in most instances. Persuasiveness or trading favors may be the onset of office politicking where you are seen as conniving and gaining support, as well as currying favor with your superiors.

WHY OFFICE POLITICS HAPPEN (3)

There are a few possible contributing factors to the increase and flourishing of office politics. Some may call them motives or hidden agendas.

1) Ambition!
   An ambitious worker is the live wire of the office. Whether an employee or employer, the ambitious person is motivated to move ahead, surpassing all others in whatever form or means, knocking out the "competition" if necessary.
   He already knows what he wants and keeps his goal constantly in his mind and heart; it may even eat into his soul to the extent that he is all consumed by it. The ambition fuels his energy and thoughts, rendering them into the appropriate actions to pave the path to move closer towards his goal. The ambitious worker may be so engrossed that he can be oblivious to others around him. He only has himself in the picture; it is his motivation.

   So here we have a very determined and highly focused worker who has laid out his plans (in his mind at least,) on achieving his goals in the arena he is in. He is full of self-confidence; ready to set in motion the plans he has worked out. His excitement fuels his passion towards the working out of his plans. As he shares his goals and plans with others, he might influence some to get on board or face some resistance. There are several ways, which this ambitious worker can take on when faced with resistance. He can pull back and re-evaluate his high-flying plans, or he might just muster more determination and push his plans forward, with whatever means to meet the goal – his *desired* goal, that is.
   There enters our foe or "friend" – office politics – through the open door of opportunity.

   How to recognize the Office Politics factor?
   A telltale sign of office politics in any ambitious person often starts when that personality has a lot of suggestions to management for "improvement". He will display his 'skills" in identifying the "problems" that cause non-productivity or backlogs. He may make specific identifications as regards to persons, situations or effects. He offers improvement alternatives.

   How does Office Politics impact its "originator" and "recipient"?
   Here, the persons in the "playing field" are the originator and the recipient(s). The originator of office politics is *the ambitious personality,* while any other person whom the ambitious personality pulls into the office politics web is the recipient.

2) Character!

Perhaps it is innate in a person, although not every person is privileged to possess it naturally. You might have encountered some colleagues or management level staff that can easily "bring a bird down from the branch." These are such influential and lively personalities that all ears and eyes are captivated when these personalities speak or make a move.

These personalities are usually eloquent, making others feel good or inferior (and finding it acceptable), as well as offering good suggestions for the betterment of the company, which are irrefutable.

They are every top brass' "P.A." and their opinions and comments are valued. They are the life of the party. Yet, we do not know if such personalities will use their "gift" wisely and fairly or otherwise. A word of suggestion from these may just turn your working world upside down, even if you have been in their "clique."

How to recognize the Office Politics Personality:
This is a very amiable person. He has the ability to put people at their ease, especially those at the higher level of management. He is good at creating conditions that feature himself, and that portray him as the right person for the job. He can draw co-workers into discussions, and share just enough information in order to gain information from others. He is a good listener and possibly, a problem solver.

How does Office Politics impact its "originator" and "recipient"?
The originator of office politics is *the influential personality*; the one who is more outspoken and bold; the one who offers the "bright ideas." The *recipient* of office politics has been influenced by the dominant worker.

3) Fear!

Fear is either a great motivator or a great crippler of a person. Let's take a look at the latter first. If fear grips you to such an extent that it stifles your productivity, you will easily and quickly end up as a "victim," be it bullied, scapegoat status, closet broom or cold storage, or shown the exit.

On the other hand, if fear motivates you, you'll feed on its energy to increase yours. You'll fear nothing and no one, and you will be able to push yourself forward to reach for your goal – in this case, your job. In a sense, you'd have lost some of your identity as there is now this "associate" backing you in your every plan or move.

You'll find yourself more forceful with people and become bolder in your moves. You would not think twice about the person you might be impacting with your words or action.

There may a change in your character. Your "associate" will invite another "accomplice" – the office politics – to assist you in your quest.

In either case, it is the attitude "each [wo]man for her/himself" that takes priority. Now is the time to seize the day, waiting or creating the "right" opportunity to grab what benefits you before another. As the saying goes, "the early bird catches the worm."

How to recognize the Office Politics factor?
This profile is hardest to recognize as the personality can be quite adept at covering his moves, or at empathizing with others. Only through experience can one identify this kind, but sometimes it may be too late. He may be the most dangerous kind of office politics originator, for he may be the "wolf in sheep's clothing."

How does Office Politics impact its "originator" and "recipient"?
The originator of office politics is then the "wolf" or *the fear-motivated personality*, while any other person who is "mauled" in the process is the recipient. There will usually be casualties. The recipient is considered the 'scapegoat" marked for sacrifice.

Truly, no worker is safe from the effects of office politics. Casualties may abound if the involved parties are not strong in the cases, or wise to the opposition. Office politics will change the atmosphere of the work place causing distrust, cliques and deception. Productivity can be badly affected if the situation is not curbed quickly or handled wisely. It takes a farsighted and wise personality to handle the position appropriately.

EXAMPLES OF OFFICE POLITICS (4)

Let us now consider some examples of Office Politics. It may seem prevalent but, it is, in reality, very insidious in any office environment. Workers know it exists and yet, seem oblivious to it at the same time. So, what form does Office Politics take on? How does it first surface?

a. Scenario 1 – Unfairness

It is frustrating when you note how certain workers just seem to have it all! They come in late and go home early with little work done, but get a raise at the end of the year. They are not reprimanded when they do not abide by the work rules and ethics and yet, they enjoy the same or more benefits than those who slogged and went the extra mile. How could that be?

b. Scenario 2 – Unethical Practices

Workers in certain positions or departments receive "fringe benefits" or appreciation gifts from outside sources such as suppliers and service providers as they were recommended for a job or tender. These are called getting "kickbacks" from external parties for using them. Workers in the company take on a dual role as a middle agent between the company and the external provider. Benefits can range from monetary commissions to holiday perks and expensive gifts.

c. Scenario 3 – Favoritism

It is a blatant abuse of power when some workers are preferred over others, and conditions of work have been adjusted to suit the favored workers. The better conditions are usually inclined towards the favored category while the "not-in-the-clique" category gets the leftovers.
This is especially frustrating when the favored workers are subordinates.

d. Scenario 4 – Malicious Gossip

I was once the subject of gossip, and the gossip was that I was rude to a sales rep, and that I called her useless and stupid. This was not true. The information went all the way up to my CEO, and my boss questioned me about it, which was how I got to know about it. I later went to the sales representative whom I called 'stupid" and clarified any misunderstanding to her. The sales rep was on my side, so she clarified things for me to the management. The best way to clear malicious gossip is to get to the source of the problem and clear the air.

e. Scenario 5 – The Trump Card

A worker threatens to resign unless his or her work conditions change. It may be a subtle or direct demand of change with the worker 'supposedly" holding the trump card. This is a very dangerous form of Office Politics as it may very well backfire against the issuer as the top management may call your bluff. The involved worker must really know how to play his trump card carefully as there may be unforeseen developments or intrinsic factors unknown to him, which may not work to his benefit. As the saying goes, "No one is indispensable." Most of the time, it is hard to retract a resignation intention, especially if it is a physical submission, such as a letter.

f. Scenario 6 – Manipulation

The worker goes about paving the path with the intention to exploit. For example, he has prior knowledge of some upcoming event, which he uses to his own advantage. The action could be just verbal where he would share information, or it could be that changes could be employed to prove his worthiness. He does whatever he can to ensure that his position in the company is not jeopardized and if possible, to position him in such a way that he will be noted as outstanding or 'savior" of the situation or problem.

g. Scenario 7 – Scratching One Another's Back

This type of Office Politics occurs when the involved parties (it could be more than 2) have this "agreement" to watch out for one another to ensure their own survival. They work together to cover up for each other to avoid office discipline. For example, a worker may have gone off earlier than the normal work hours but the "accomplice" will offer a palatable excuse to cover for his absence, so that he will not be viewed unfavorably by management.

h. Scenario 8 – Backstabbing

A worker finds himself being called up by the management to account for some decisions made or actions done to the disadvantage of the organization. It could be a case of an employee being accused by other colleagues of misusing his authority, when, in fact, the accused was not privy to the accusation until the matter becomes full blown, with management stepping in.

i. Scenario 9 – Hypocrisy

A worker may react like a chameleon wherein he adjusts himself to the company he is with at the moment. He may have a very versatile character that allows him to modify himself to the current environment to find favor with those around him, especially those with authority or in power.

j. Scenario 10 – Whistle-Blowing

A supervisor shares, in confidence, that he has a better job offer that is tempting him to move on from the current company. An employee who got wind of it relays news of his possible exit from the company to the management. The supervisor is called up and reprimanded upon questioning.

HOW TO MAKE OFFICE POLITICS WORK FOR YOU (5)

There is always more than one solution to any problem; overcoming Office Politics is no different. Any suggested 'solution" is dependent on the recipient's moral or ethical values, principles or philosophical mentality. It could also be guided by one's spiritual ethos.

Here are some suggested solutions to make office politics work for you instead of against you. There is not a right or wrong solution offered here, but each suggested solution is just one way where one might take on dealing with the problem at hand. There may be other suggested solutions to one particular scenario taken up.

Whether the world economy improves or not, office politics will be around as long as man is around. It is the survival of the fittest, really. Man's innate being will go on "auto-mode" to survive, unless he has some other focus or priority; otherwise, it's a "man-eat-man" world.

This section also looks at the two different perspectives on an office politicking state of affairs – from the point of view of a victim and the advocator. The victim is the person who feels he has been unjustly involved in that particular office politics trait, while the advocator is the person who has exercised the office politics trait.

a. Scenario 1 – Unfairness

Unfairness is common at the office. When this kind of situation surfaces, one might want to "play smart" by getting on the good side of the authority. Consider being a "pal" with your superior; that is, establishing good relations with your manager, and you are able to get away with a few misdeeds or misdemeanors because of the "good" ties you have set. For example, you are able to go home earlier when you "have a word" with your superior on an urgent or important need or task to perform outside the office.

You may even enjoy certain "perks" or privileges which are not in the "book" or office rules and regulations, as your superior can "override" these unlisted actions such as being part of the lunch party for a supplier or client, some of which seem petty and trivial while some are "expected."

It is up to your supervisor's discretion to authorize you or anyone whom he/she deems deserving or favored to be given the "privilege." Hence, to overcome the frustration of seeing other colleagues "having a ball," you can also join the bandwagon with a little "politics handling." As the saying goes, "If you can't beat them, join them," provided no malice is intended and no law is flouted.

Some at the office may look upon some of these practices as unfair, while they may actually be situations where a superior can be "flexible" in exercising his or her authority to bring the best or further potential of the workers.

Which side of the fence are you on?
Unfairness

Side 1: The Victim or Observer

If you are on this side of the fence, then you really need to view the situation very carefully to identify the reason(s) you are receiving the shorter end of the stick. Was it your previous misdemeanor that caused a "fallout" with your department, colleagues or superiors that you feel you are being unfairly treated? Is it a miscommunication or misunderstood scenario as you are not privy to the details of the circumstances? Before you go lashing out at the presumed unfair practice, you would be wise to investigate the cause and effect first. It could very well be a minor issue that has been blown out of proportion without careful thought and evaluation.

Side 2: The Advocator

If you receive feedback on your **alleged** unfair practices, you would do well to sit down and evaluate the situation carefully, identifying any truth to the **allegations**, feedback or gossip. You might be the last to know but when you do know, it would be good to have a self-check to ensure that there is no truth to the allegations so that you can continue with your productivity and good performance in the company without fear or stress that someone may report you to management at any time.

If you are able to identify the source of the allegations, you may want to consider inviting the source to engage in an open and mature discussion with an aim towards resolving the issue.

Why should you work with a dark cloud over you when the allegations are untrue?

Should there be some truth in the allegations, you should consider the pros and cons really seriously so that you are motivated to stop the unfair practices and stop the allegations. Try to work well with all those around you to enhance the productivity, instead of being slanted towards those who curry favors for you, even in subtle ways, such as getting your coffee or buying you lunch or gifts.

b. Scenario 2 – Unethical Practices

Every worker loves "fringe benefits" or "kickbacks"; it is human nature to receive than to give. Receiving makes most people feel good, feel appreciated and noted of their very existence. To call a gift that is a token of appreciation a kickback is a bit too harsh. People who perform well need some encouragement to keep them motivated and keep performing or outperforming themselves. Gifts are motivation to perform. That is the reason for bonuses or increments, and the bigger the paycheck, the happier you feel, don't you? You'd say "I deserve it, for I have worked hard the whole year, contributing to the company's healthy finances." Companies offer dividends and ESOS to their employees when they perform well each year. Are these unethical? So then, if you accept these fringe benefits or bonuses from your companies at the end of the year for the work done or outstanding performance, what of the "tokens of appreciation" from outside sources?

Suppliers and service providers are also humans wanting to make a living; they need some "assistance" to make it through the "difficult times" of their business. They require "a break" or an opportunity to move on from their business stagnancy. So, who is going to give them the opportunity they need to prove their worthiness? Competition is stiff; they need a chance to show their capability. Man is very creative and innovative; he will "create" the opportunity even when none comes his way. Man is impatient; he has to overcome that hurdle before it trips him. The "giver" is fighting for survival too, have you thought of that? Every man for himself; the supplier or service provider wants more trade to make his business viable and to survive in this competitive world, so he "offers" some kind of incentive to the "insider" who may "assist." As the saying goes, "every man has a price." If the price is right, the "deal" goes through.

When the supplier or provider is more desperate in securing the tender or job, the higher or more attractive the offer will be. This is where the "unethical" practices of work or business come into play.

Which side of the fence are you on?
Unethical practices

Side 1: The Victim or Observer
You are feeling or observing such practices at the office. It is often difficult to label unethical practices precisely as "one man's meat is another man's poison." So, if you feel that you are observing or experiencing unethical practices at the office, you will need to identify what constitutes an unethical practice at your workplace for it could be deemed "an office culture" such as everyone is expected to contribute to the boss' birthday, anniversary and other special occasions.

Side 2: The Advocator
If you might be practicing unethical maneuvers at the office, or are informed so, you should consider the damage caused through these unethical practices; on one's self, colleagues, department and company.
When the offer is going to cause unfair advantage to one party, then it is best not to be party to that practice for negative innuendoes may come creeping up on you. There is so much more to lose in the long run than to enjoy the "benefit" for the short term, unless you are really desperate

or willing to take a large risk. It is hard to halt the practices as more and more enticing offers may come your way. And once you are "found out," your reputation will be ripped into shreds, beyond repair. So, is it worth the risk?

c. Scenario 3 – Favoritism

The "green-eyed monster" comes on in us when we see others being preferred over ourselves. Such is the nature of man. What can you do when you feel others around you, yes, even subordinates, seem to be more preferred or favored over yourself?

Many on the sidelines will cry "favoritism;" perhaps so, perhaps not. Perhaps it is a case of misunderstanding the situation, or even "the grass looks greener at the other side;" it always does. We may think that certain people are favored but maybe, just maybe, there was a "deal" cut; for example, a worker may seem to be going home early every day but maybe he was subject to a pay cut or plans to make up the hours during the weekends. One cannot jump to a conclusion from what we see or even hear; we must know the facts before we evaluate and judge. That is how the system operates.
So, with "favoritism" in the office, you would be wise to check out the true condition first. No company is ever so compassionate over an employee in any situation. There is always "payback" from what it offered to the worker. As the saying goes, "there is no such thing as a free meal," There are bound to be obligations or some expectations imposed on the employee. In the work environment, it is usually the case of "one has to sing for his supper."

Hence, favoritism needs to be clearly understood in all its aspects. Then, one can evaluate the circumstances carefully to decide whether or not he or she is willing to take on that same deal, if you want the same "favored" conditions. For example, if an employee were allowed to go home earlier every day for some reason, he must take a pay cut. Will you be willing to do so? As an employee, you have obligations to the company; you need to provide them with a stipulated number of hours per day, **for** a certain number of days in the week, and weeks and months in a year for a wage, agreed upon at hiring.

A boss or superior may exercise his or her authority to give some leeway to the employee's or subordinate's request at different times, but no boss or superior will jeopardize his or her own position to allow the employees to have an easy time at the office. Instead, a lot more would be expected of the worker who is granted some special arrangements to contribute in favor of the company.

Each worker or employee has his or her own commitments or moral values. Will your current priority allow you to make the changes to gain the "favors" because in the real competitive world, favoritism in the office is like an "I-owe-U; "payback" is always expected in full, sooner or later. So, make a wise calculated risk before you venture into it.

Which side of the fence are you on?
Favoritism

Side 1: The Victim

If you are a "victim" of this type of office politics, you will feel unfairness that you are not as highly regarded as others at the workplace and may query yourself what is it that you lack which others have? It could be personality or character which you may have to decide to change if you want to be included in the clique, or it could be a past misdemeanor of yours that has caused you to be alienated from the group or superior.

You can eat a little bit of humble pie and seek an open and honest discussion with the relevant authority to understand the unfavorable situation that you find yourself in, or just bite the bullet and carry on with all the dignity you can muster to concentrate on your job. Hopefully your good performance will not go unnoticed by upper management. Perhaps your good performance might even win you over to the favorite category. Sometimes it is difficult for newcomers to the office environment to be fully accepted by the veterans until they warm up to the novices or have sized the newcomers up thoroughly. Most of the time, veterans are quite comfortable among themselves and may prove quite defensive to allow new employees into their "nest."

Side 2: The Advocator

If you are practicing favoritism in an authoritative position, you might want to query your own actions. For the sake of your career and reputation in the long run, is this current practice worthwhile or should there be quick changes made to your benefit? As with the stock market, it cannot enjoy or sustain a run for too long, much less all the time. Self-provoking questions such as is it necessary to show favoritism to some and not to others, and should your show of favoritism be so blatant that it riles up others, should be asked to check your own conscience. These questions can serve to safeguard your current position if you heed to the need to change, for nothing remains constant. As the saying goes, "the only constant is change."

A deeper thought-provoking question is, "will there be any supporters for you should your position spiral down?" to consider the continuing practice of favoritism.

d. Scenario 4 – Malicious Gossip

There are bound to be gossips at the workplace; it may be just a casual exchange of news or happenings in the office, or it may be a deliberate instigation – one with a malicious intent, while others may be harmless.
Since no one is an island on this earth, every employee or worker in the workplace should learn to interact with one another, whether on a professional level or a more friendly nature, if personalities click well. This will help reduce any talk of you, especially eliminating the malicious rumors, unless you have overstepped your work boundaries along the way.

A gossip may be a fleeting comment from another with no second thought or deliberation or even desire to explore the comment further, while other kinds of gossip are fanned into flames. One must be bold in dealing with gossips at the workplace, especially when the gossip concerns oneself or when the gossip is blatantly untrue.

If you hear a rumor about yourself, be calm and do not overreact. Try to find out more about the full contents, implications, source and the path taken without being emotional; put on a professional front. Take on the investigation with a clear mind so as to not cloud your understanding of the information gathered or cause you to "jump the gun" too early.

If it is an untrue report which you have knowledge of, it is good to "update" the "informer" of the actual situation in order to stop the gossip in its tracks. If it is gossip about another worker, you can either stop it from spreading by letting the information stop with you, or you can convey your concerns to the right authority for the appropriate action to be taken so that the gossip will not be allowed to fan its flames to a greater volume. Someone has to douse the fire, so they say. Who will be the office firefighter?

To keep gossips in check at the workplace, one must be discerning to the type of gossip that is conveyed. As mentioned, it may be an innocent fleeting comment passed as a joke that stops right there at the circle, or it may be an intentional instigation or a simple misgiving that is blown out of proportion as it makes its way around the office.

If you are a superior, you might want to keep your eyes and ears open to be aware of the changes happening in the office environment so that any unproductive vibes can be dealt with immediately. As the Chinese saying goes, "pull out the roots totally to prevent re-growth of the weeds." If you are in a position of authority, keeping the office atmosphere free from gossips will be a healthier environment for your workers' increased productivity.

Perhaps that is one of the reasons for more work assigned to the employees, so that they will have less time to gossip, which can reduce office productivity.

Which side of the fence are you on?
Malicious gossip

Side 1: The Victim

Gossips about you may or may not come back to haunt you. Either way, it can be detrimental to your reputation. You might be carrying on with your work and wondering why some people are acting in such a hostile manner towards you when you have not interacted with them at all. They have already "heard news" of you and have formed their own (unfavorable) view of you. Here, you will need to have strong and good principles to carry you through, as there is nothing much you can do if you are not made aware of the situation against you. Only time will tell if you walk righteously.

When the gossip comes back to you, you can activate the corrective plan to set the situation right. Perhaps it was a miscommunication or misunderstanding of some words or actions conveyed by you to another. Gossip tends to be blown out of proportion when it goes from one person to another. You may wish to calmly identify the source of the gossip to have a professional and calm discussion so that any contention can be eased and resolved amicably. Forgiving one another to move on is the best path to take, since all parties are still colleagues at the workplace.

Alternatively, you can refer the issue to your superior if the allegations are untrue or to clarify the issue if there is any slight tinge of truth in the gossip. It is essential to remain pleasant and professional about the whole issue so that no one can label you as "cry baby" as you run to your boss with the issue. But if the gossip is malicious, it is necessary to clear your involvement or reputation before it goes any further.

Side 2: The Advocator

If you are the source or perpetrator of the malicious gossip on another, it is a mature move to reconsider your actions. Have a self-check on the cause of the gossip and take positive steps in gaining good closure rather than letting it run wild around the office. **Could your action stem from a misunderstanding that occurred in the past between you and the person spreading the rumors?** No one by nature would really want to avenge themselves unless they have been deeply hurt or angered by another, and it could be a pure misunderstanding. Why let the spite eat away at your good nature and conscience because of one person, one bad deed or some unkind words? There is no real need for a "tit-for-tat" unless it is a good deed. When you have been hurt, your forgiving nature will be open for all to see and admire, and you will gain more than a good reputation, friends and career prospects. You gain self-esteem and purity, which are not easy to achieve in this hard world.

e. Scenario 5 – The Trump Card

The Trump card is a dangerous form of Office Politics which can make or break its dealer. You may think you have something of worth in your hand, but unless you are the boss or privy to the whole office or business strategy, you may be burned if you handle the trump card precariously.

No worker is indispensable in this time or era of economy where competition is stiff amongst businesses who expect more of the workers within an organization. Threats to resign may not work to your favor or expectations nowadays, including even the threat of en-block resignation. With the ailing or not-so-favorable economy, there are many who would be happy to move into your position, even if at a lower remuneration.

Your threat to resign unless your conditions for work are met may miss its mark as the higher management may have already anticipated your moves and are prepared for you. Thus, instead of a trump card, it may backfire.

If you are holding the trump card and want to throw it out to your advantage, you'd need to be very sure of the other players' cards first. They may have better trump cards than yours, and you'd end up the loser. It is always better to go easy with the ultimatum – better to be safe than sorry. Check and double-check your facts, as well as evaluate all pros and cons of your trump card decision before acting on it. Getting some third party opinion on the situation is helpful for a fresh and unbiased point of view. These outsourced assistance or counsel should be received with an open mind, however, in order to benefit you in viewing the conditions from another perspective before dealing your trump card.

Sometimes there is no turning back when dealing the trump card. It is like "opening a can of worms" that has been kept under control for a long time, and no one wants to kick up the dust, until you do. You have to consider the trump card option extremely cautiously before taking action on it.

Which side of the fence are you on?
Using the Trump Card

Side 1: The Victim
When someone uses a trump card on you, it means that you are held at their mercy. They have a hold on you that can cause your downfall at the office; sometimes it is construed as some form of "blackmail" or political coercion. It is likened to "do as I say or else…" It may be a soft threat or persuasion that obliges you to conform to the request of the trump card holder. It is unforeseeable that a good colleague or boss might turn on you when the situation gets tough. You might be forced into a corner and give in lamely because your reputation or career is on the line. For example, you might have shared with a colleague who is supposedly very close to you that you did not quite finish your studies but managed to get the certificate, and now you and your colleague are up for promotion. Your colleague might use this information against you

hoping that you will step aside to secure her/his position for promotion, especially if she/he feels that you are a strong contender for the promotion. Hence, to avoid becoming a victim of trump card advocators, do not release sensitive information to your closest colleague. It can turn against you in the future.

Side 2: The Advocator

The person who uses the trump card usually thinks he has an upper hand on the situation or person. He assumes he has relevant and important information that might give him some mileage in his pursuit of success at the office. For example, he may threaten the company with resignation and taking the whole department with him if his request of promotion is not met. His intention is to coerce management into appeasing him with his demand as he assumes he is quite indispensable or a great asset to the company. But sometimes, the trump card advocator may have his plan backfire, as the management may call his bluff and be willing to release him. With the tough competition for jobs in the ailing economy, the management may be willing to use this opportunity to release the perhaps long-serving but now demanding employee to get someone younger and less expensive to take over. It is a good opportunity for companies to downsize in a competitive industry. Hence, the trump card advocator should be careful in using the trump card, as it could have adverse repercussions if not all angles of the issue have been researched thoroughly. If you want to use the trump card, you must be sure that you really have a winning hand.

f. Scenario 6 – Manipulation

Manipulation is a common routine of life, not just in the office. When one offers another something in exchange for a favor or some assistance, it is manipulation whether the second party knows about the intent or not. When you want to gain by changing the conditions, it is manipulation.

Some might consider this move as shrewd, adjusting the situation or conditions, or enlisting willing parties to make something benefit you. Others see it as 'seizing the opportunity,' as they view an opening or the chance to turn an event or situation to their favor. So, manipulation can be viewed as "creating the opportunity" or 'seizing the opportunity;' either way, alertness is a trait of the manipulator. He is always on the lookout and when he plays his role well, he succeeds.

In the office environment, there are many circumstances that one could "manipulate" in order to gain mileage for self or for the organization. Being a crony is one way to manipulate. Relations are another, as favor is usually slanted to its own kind. As the saying goes, "birds of a feather flock together."

To succeed in office politics manipulation, one needs to be alert, keeping your eyes and ears to the "ground" and "walls", awaiting opportunities to arise – smelling the "first whiff of blood" so they say, or striking while the iron is hot! It is like getting rumors of an impending rise in the stock market and you are ready to put your stake on it for a fast and sure win. Charm is switched on, along with some finesse, for a convincing take, as it maneuvers like a non-threatening activity on its unsuspecting prey. It is often quietly exercised to prevent any uproar that might not be favorable.

But nothing is guaranteed in life; the same for manipulation. It takes a lot of effort and time to stay watchful and something else usually gives way when one is concentrating on and being watchful for "opportunities." Health or work performance may suffer, unless that opportunity really comes knocking on your door.

When manipulation is badly handled, the pitfalls set in. Your reputation suffers and it can be quite difficult to climb back up or stand tall again. It is like being declared "bankrupt" when you have little or no means and resources to settle your outstanding bills.

Manipulation functions very much like the stock market; you can make big bucks or you can get burned. You can gain or you can lose along the way. You must know how to 'salvage' yourself should you fall through with the manipulation.

Which side of the fence are you on?
Manipulation

Side 1: The Victim
The victim of manipulation is usually on the receiving end, which could be viewed as good or bad. Yes, he receives "goodies" from the advocator, but some return or favor is expected, either now or in the future. The victim should be cautious when receiving gifts and offerings from anyone related to work, as it could be an obligation on you for a return of assistance sometime later. For example, your boss might be treating you to lunch this month, but next month, he expects you to stay late to work on a project without allowances or overtime. You would feel obligated to his request as he fed you the previous month. Hence, no matter how small or insignificant the offer or gift may be, it may be the start of manipulation, which you might not be aware of. When you have received too much, it is extremely hard for you to say "no" to any request made of you unless you resign from the company.

Side 2: The Advocator
The advocator may be a superior or a very close colleague who works well with others. If you need the assistance of your colleagues or subordinates, it is better to go by the book than to manipulate. There may be new workers who feel obliged to meet your demands or requests as they may feel threatened in their job security if they fail to comply, but there are those who think they are in for a joy ride. However, it is not ethical to manipulate people by obliging them with

gifts and favors for a return of the same or more at a later time. If it is work-related, you can always request or instruct your subordinates or colleagues to cooperate for the good of the company and motivate them for a good performance or increased productivity.

If you really appreciate a colleague or subordinate, then you can offer a token of appreciation for a job well done with no strings attached; Alternatively, you can recommend the responsible employee for a raise or promotion at the year-end appraisal. These are proper channels, which one can take on without any form or hint of manipulation. It should not be a case of "if I promote you, then you need to help me when I call on you." No one is a slave to anyone else at the workplace; all are hired for his or her own role and task. Manipulation should not exist in the office, for there are many proper channels through which a superior can use to reward or discipline, unless the superior wants some personal benefits or has some personal agenda for which he wants some "runners" in the office. It could also be in the form of office moles from one department to another.

Manipulation causes distrust and stress, as the victim is to be at the "beck and call" of the advocator. The advocator acts like the "king" with his small or influential "kingdom" of supporters at the office. One possible manipulation advocator could be the union head, who might influence the union members to go out on strike when making promotion or salary increase demands to the company.

g. Scenario 7 – Scratching Each Other's Back

No one is an island; not even in the office. You're bound to get on well with some colleague(s), with whom you would form an "affiliation" with some implied loyalty invested into it. The same may be said of your colleagues in that same group, as with other groups in the office. It could be your lunch partner or project team. It could be your department colleagues or anyone who shares the same interest or focus point.

Cliques form because of the comfort or security its members feel in each other's presence or with one another. There may be some common areas of interests or personalities, which attract one to the other to form a clique.

Cliques in the office environment are quite protective over its "members". The members tend to cover up for one another, as well as to inform for the members' benefit. This kind of back scratching is quite the opposite of another kind of office politics: backstabbing.

Scratching one another's back in the office makes one feel comforted, valued and secure. It is a good practice in the office if it is properly administered. Members tend to have an unwritten code of conduct that protects and cares for one another in the affiliation. They spend a lot of time together in the office, especially during lunch hours, and may even extend to outside office hours. Sometimes the affiliation may have some obligations from members. It is like being in the labor union. There may or may not be a "leader" for the group, but information and advice abound that are privy to the group members.

It is good to be in an affiliation of some kind (hopefully, the right kind) as no one has eyes in the back of their head, nor can anyone be everywhere all time. One cannot be alert to everything in the office, but members of the group may be in the right place at the right time. They can share information, which many will construe as gossiping, but that is part of human nature. The information network administered by cliques can be quite amazing!

Cliques can grow to be very strong bonds of relationships that can last a long time. Leaving a clique is not impossible, but it can leave a bad taste in your mouth, so to speak, especially if you have been affiliated for quite some time. But it can and does happen. Departure from the clique may be necessary due to fallouts of relationships, promotions or resignations.

Hence, it is advisable to seek out the right clique to be involved in or to be affiliated so that it benefits you. As the saying goes, "bad company corrupts," your choice of cliques in the office either benefits or harms you.

Which side of the fence are you on?
Scratching each other's back

Side 1: The Victim
The victim gets relief when his back is scratched, or when someone does a favor for him; stress is reduced and productivity levels can be maintained. It could be a one-off occasion that requires support; an emergency or a planned occasion that requires secrecy from management's knowledge. The victim must trust his accomplice 100%, believing that he will not be played out by his partner.

Side 2: The Advocator
The advocator is the **one who does favors for another person in the hope of having the favor returned**. He is usually a willing participant, as he knows that the occasion will arise when the favor is reciprocated; that is the motivation. As an advocator, one must be sure of the risks involved, as you are the first party to be questioned over the other party's misconduct at the office. Care must be taken over the words used to convey a favorable response to the superiors, or anyone else, to avoid discipline or ill-favor of the management or superiors.

It is sometimes difficult to identify who is the victim and who is the advocator in this situation, as usually both are willing parties whose roles will interchange. It has been mutually agreed to watch out for each other and to cover for each other wherever there is a need, so that one or the other does not get into trouble with the management.

Physically, everyone knows that having your back scratched is a great feeling of relief. You feel good and so you are a willing party. In office politicking, it is similar with assisting one another. You will want to find a good and willing accomplice, so to speak, for this task. This responsibility works well with a pair or trio. More than that becomes a crowd and the support may not be as strong or loyal between one another. Someone usually gets left out when the group is too big. Like the saying goes, "three is a crowd." It is easier to coordinate between two persons, or at most, three, than more. Similar personalities make better partners in office politicking as they are more attuned to the preferences of their partner because they share common traits.

So, in this way, they are victim and advocator, as both are willing parties to the game until a fallout. It is very difficult to separate the pair unless there is a row between them. A strong third party or a change of interest like a promotion or transfer of department might just do the trick to break up this office politicking trait.

h. Scenario 8 – Backstabbing

Backstabbing, or criticizing someone while feigning friendship, should be a rare occurrence in the office as there are many other options in playing office politics. It can happen if one employee has been discredited by another and wishes to take some form of revenge. Although we do not have eyes behind us, as the saying goes, you might need to "watch your back" if you do not wish to be a victim of this type of betrayal. This would mean being careful of your words and actions at the office which another might take offense at, and may consider revenge in some form, such as instigation or setting a trap for your downfall at work.

A backstabber would probably be one who is very unhappy or dissatisfied with a person or situation at work that has caused undue embarrassment or discredit to the self. Revenge is one reason for underhanded behavior, while a really bad attitude could be another; perhaps in an effort to climb up the ladder, the backstabber needs to clear "the competition" in order to shine before the authorities for credit and promotion.

Someone who is going to metaphorically stab you in the back is quite a devious person. They would go to some lengths in order to gain your trust, e.g. pretending to be your friend. Once your trust has been obtained, and your guard lowered, it becomes very easy to deceive you by harassment, spreading untrue gossip and the like.

Another way to overcome backstabbing is to confront it; should you get to know of it, and especially if it is with regards to you, you should confront the originator for clarification. It is better to have the issue out in the open than to try to be manipulative. When the issue is handled in the open, it is there for all to hear, see and evaluate; you might even get some sympathetic votes or support. Perhaps the management will be forced to step in to clear the situation, a good thing as there should be closure on such situations, which are never healthy for the organization or its employees. When the issue is dealt with in the open, there is no room for further deception and manipulation; and all involved parties will be on their toes to react carefully as the issue is now public and the management is taking an interest.

In contrast, if you are the originator, you would be better off in staying calm and rational over the issue. You should be very clear of your actions and line of reasoning as you might need to account for the uncouth action on your colleague. Though backstabbing may happen subtly, it rears an ugly head if it is forced into the open.

As prevention is better than cure, it is better to avoid harassing your colleagues in the first place to achieve your ambition. There are many ways to skin a cat, and being professional about any office issue is the best step forward, as it augurs well with all parties, especially yourself, for your professionalism will put you in the forefront of respectability and credibility.

Which side of the fence are you on?
Backstabbing

Side 1: The Victim
As in a crime scene, the "injured" victim is usually the unknowing person not watching his back; hence, he got stabbed in the back. It is a sad case as no one has eyes in the back of their head, and it is tedious and stressful to be always turning around to check who is creeping up behind. A victim could have stepped onto someone's toes without knowing and thus, is targeted for revenge. He could also be deemed as an easy prey for a project gone awry, for which a scapegoat is required as a 'sacrifice" to appease the management.

Side 2: The Advocator
The advocator could be someone holding a deep grudge and waits for "payback" time to the victim who may have caused embarrassment or trouble to **the untrustworthy advocator**. The advocator may set his trap slowly, building his web of deceit or camouflaging his trap carefully to avoid detection and ensuring success. The unwitting victim falls into the trap if he is not careful. Hence, the advocator will have a field day when he catches his victim unaware, who falls from grace clueless of the cause, feeling only the bad effects. The advocator is shrewd in his set up, needing to ensure that he is not seen to have done anything wrong even if he is found out, because he would have been quite thorough in his plans beforehand. It is usually the unknowing victim that suffers most in this situation. Unless there is strong support for the victim, either through his colleagues or superiors, it is difficult to survive an attack of this nature in office politics. Alternatively, the management undertakes a thorough investigation and takes an unbiased stance on the case until a complete inquiry is performed. Usually the company does not wish to waste its time, resources and personnel on such matters if it concerns only one or two employees. The management may just write the case off with a resignation unless the reputation of the company is at stake or a huge sum of funds is involved.

i. Scenario 9 – Hypocrisy

A hypocrite is a person who shows him/herself differently to different people, or is someone who is nice to you in person but may speak badly of you behind your back, or one who changes his story according to the circumstances as time goes by. A hypocrite's actions and words are inconsistent; hence, one would need to be very careful around a hypocrite.

Firstly, you need to identify the hypocrite. You must check his words and actions through other people, as a hypocrite would say different things to different people. If his words and actions are proven to be inconsistent or fluffed with air and excuses (which are usually cover-ups for his lies), then it is best to stay away from such a person or be alert and on your guard when interacting with this person. Do not indulge in personal or important information with the hypocrite as he may manipulate your input to his advantage, or worse, to your disadvantage.

It is best to be superficial with the hypocrite, keeping your distance and displaying your professionalism in handling or interacting with him, no matter how sweet and charming he can be.

A hypocrite in the office may seem to be good company, who lends his or her ears readily (for he or she may be trying to source information out of you!) This character may be quite sympathetic, but do not accept everything he or she says or does, no matter how convincing it all may seem, for there is a possibility of a "trap" somewhere. Always take what he or she offers with a pinch of salt in order to safeguard yourself. Wisdom shall be proven true in due time.

If you are new to the office, keep a professional front and find out the true characters of your colleagues before you open yourself up to anyone. Keen observation and asking around will help you in your task so that you'd know who the "wolf in sheep's clothing" is.

Hypocrisy is a matter of character. Once a person's character is set, it is quite difficult to change him or her. Hence, one needs to be wise and alert, or perhaps be a good judge of character, to avoid the pit of hypocrisy.

Which side of the fence are you on?
Hypocrisy

Side 1: The Victim
The Chinese saying, "put on your glasses to view the person properly" holds some truth with this hypocrisy trait of office politicking. A victim of hypocrisy is caused by his inability to differentiate the true and false friends or colleagues. In simpler words, he has been played out or betrayed. He could have been in good company at the beginning but people do change even if the leopard does not change its spots! What caused the victim's betrayal could be many reasons – he

was not really a true friend anyway. He was just being used until an appropriate time when he was of some value, like a pawn to be sacrificed. The victim could have fallen out of grace with the advocator or he didn't know the advocator's true identity at all. He was taken in from start to finish. Yes, the advocator could have projected himself as a good friend at the beginning, but with the stress and competition at work, anything can change a good friendship.

Hypocrisy can happen to the victim very quickly depending on the situation. If the advocator is pressed hard, he will very likely act like the chameleon, changing quickly to suit his surroundings. And if that is not sufficient to defend himself for survival, hypocrisy can arise at the expense of his close and trusting friends or colleagues.

For example, the hypocrite may agree to participate in a sit-out against management's bad practices but change his mind and is seen to be standing on management's side due to fear of loss of job or has possibly been bought over by management.

Side 2: The Advocator

The advocator of hypocrisy is the hypocrite. He could react on the spur of the moment in a desperate attempt to save his own skin, or he could have planned his words and actions. He usually reacts to fear and intimidation or to a strong ambition to succeed, at every other person's expense. He can be ruthless in that way. He will manipulate to benefit his ambition, even if it means exploiting others through a change of support through words or deeds.

Being ambitious is good when realizing your potential, but it should not be at another's expense. Today, someone may need your help but there will be a time when you will need someone else's help. Hence, it is not wise to toy with hypocrisy as it is detrimental to your reputation and to your future. You will lose friends fast and you will end up very lonely and unhappy, no matter how successful you are. Worse still, people who have identified your characteristic will target you the same way or never be true friends to you.

When you practice hypocrisy, you are burning all ropes of friendship and trust, and trust when destroyed, is very hard to rebuild. Learn to say what you mean, and mean what you say, sticking by it through thick and thin, or else, think before you speak to avoid difficult situations where you cannot retract your words or promises.

j. Scenario 10 – Whistle-Blowing

A whistle-blower is not appreciated by anyone in the company, although the management might seemingly welcome such characters to provide "grassroots" news. It is likened to a mole in the workplace, although not all whistle-blowers have that unkind intention. Some whistle-blowers may just want the right action to be taken instead of allowing possible unfair practices to happen. For example, the given scenario of the employee who overheard news that his supervisor may be moving on to a better paid job and reporting it to management may be having several concerns.

A whistle-blower is quite an opportunist. He keeps his ears and eyes open for news, which he may report to the higher authorities to gain a notch on the ladder for himself.

He is eager to be in the know of things at the workplace but can disguise his intentions if he is cunning and shrewd in his actions.

In the scenario given, the whistle-blower could be harboring malicious intent against the supervisor and thus, acted maliciously to inform the management. Or he is concerned about the workflow of the company with the supervisor considering leaving the company, which can distract him from his current responsibilities and work performance quality. If you were caught in such a position, it is best to stay calm and investigate the matter thoroughly before taking any action, favorable or otherwise. If you are not part of the affected party, it is best to stay out of the situation instead of being drawn in at any point in any way. There will be enough concerned people who will keep a keen eye on the matter.

Which side of the fence are you on?
Whistle-blowing

Side 1: The Victim
The victim will feel very annoyed with the whistle-blower if the identity is known, or frustrated if the identity is not made known. Distrust will arise towards most people around him and that is not healthy for oneself and others. He will eventually leave the company because of the embarrassment and distrust towards others. Even if the identity is known and the matter is openly discussed and resolved, the damage is already done to the victim, unless management does not pursue the matter. But the distrust will be hard to dispel after the incident and there is bound to be enmity between the two parties.

Side 2: The Advocator
One must always take a bird's eye view of the situation before taking any action. If you were the whistle-blower, you should have checked out the facts first. After all, the supervisor did not formalize his intention to leave the company. All employees have the right to consider a higher-paying post or a better job with another company if there are little or no progressive opportunities at the current workplace. Hence, one should not rob another of the chance to progress or move forward in his career. Envy and spite are bad attitudes to take on for any person, much less a fellow colleague. Respect should be given to the person with a possible intention to leave, and allow him the space and the right to inform management of his decision himself.

These past pages have examined office politics from the perspective of the individual, working in isolation within the office environment. What happens if this person is unable to make friends, or gather a healthy support system? To whom does he turn if he becomes a victim of office politics?

The following chapters address this very question. One does not have to cope as an individual when one has faith and God on one's side. God is the ultimate employer, and we are all his employees. There isn't a place in God's Kingdom for office politics; why should there be in our lives?

THE BIBLICAL SOLUTION TO OFFICE POLITICS (6)

I have this wonderfully cute small book of wisdom, entitled, "Man Says, God Says" which presents the differing views of Man and God in different scenarios or situations. Let us consider how God would see this situation and how He would advise in these scenarios. Be forewarned! His answers may not be what you would expect. It's already mentioned in Isaiah 55:8,9 "For My (God) thoughts are not your thoughts, neither are My ways your ways, says the Lord; for as high as the heavens are from the earth, so are My ways higher than your ways, and My thoughts your thoughts."

a. Scenario 1 – Unfairness

1 Peter 2:19 – For it is commendable if a man bears up under the pain of unfair suffering because he is conscious of God

This first scenario depicts the unfair treatment given to some staff by the superiors, making them slack at work. Other members of staff that are not in the favored grouping feel the biased treatment but can do nothing about it.

Unfairness has existed since civilization, where men fought amongst themselves to get what they want. But as God's people, we are to trust Him for all the blessings and "goodies" as promised in 2 Corinthians 9:8. "God is able to provide me with every blessing in abundance". The question then is, "Do Christians want what non-Christians want or have?" Where should our focus be?

The Bible shares a parable, which is an everyday story with lesson, in the book of Matthew that depicts "unfairness" in some people's eyes. In Matthew 20:1-16, there is a landowner who went out early in the morning to hire men to work in his vineyard. He found some and he agreed to pay them "a denarius" for the day and he sent them into his vineyard. Three hours later, he went out again and hired more workers; he did so again 3 hours later, and again in the late afternoon. An hour before the close of the workday (evening), he found some men loitering as no one had hired them. The landowner hired them right away. Finally, at the close of the workday, the hired men were called to receive their payment, beginning with those who came in latest to those who came at the beginning of the workday.

When the late workers were paid a denarius, the earlier workers were happy for they thought they would get more since they worked longer. But when their turn came to receive their wages, they were also given a denarius. They were indignant against the landowner's unfair treatment to them over those who worked less. But the landowner reasoned with them:
1) A denarius was their agreed terms of employment. (v.13)

2) They had no right to question the landowner's decision, for it is HIS money to do as HE likes or sees fit. (v.15)

Thus, the landowner kept his part of the bargain, and had acted to each hired worker according to the terms and conditions set for each one. He did no wrong to any of the workers. He was not unfair (v.13).

Lesson:
1) Unfairness is a perception. One might deem a situation unfair when the person feels his rights have been violated. But a closer look at the situation might reveal that it is not so. Man tends to be favorable towards himself and often forgets the "original terms and conditions" when he views better conditions that he wants a part of.

2) Everyone is entitled to do whatever he likes with whatever belongs to him. The observer cannot begrudge the owner of his actions. The observer can only hope that the owner will be as generous to him as he is with others, or be content as long as his own rights are not violated.

How to overcome unfairness in Office Politics
As mentioned earlier, unfairness is a perceived entity, for the nature of man is such that he favors himself over others. Man tends to ask often, "Why him, and not me?" when it comes to receiving, or "Why me, and not him?" when it comes to giving. We always want the "better deal".

So, if our heart is not taught to focus on the right things in life, life is always "unfair" to us.

b. Scenario 2 – Unethical Practices
Romans 12:17 – Do not repay anyone evil for evil. Be careful to do what is right in the eyes of everybody.

Fringe benefits! Kickbacks! Tokens of appreciation! Favors! There are even stronger terms…Greasing the hands. Bribes! There are so many terms to refer to so-called "unethical" practices. At times, it is difficult to clearly see the line between black and white. It is so fine that, at times, the giver is really genuine in offering these extras, being fully appreciative or grateful for the opportunity given, especially in businesses, which could make or break the person or company.

So how wrong is wrong in the receipt of such extras? Most of us, if not all, would have experienced such giving and receiving in our lives. The receivers feel appreciated and the "extra" is helpful in molding a better life; a more comfortable one; that is the desire of man.

In the book of Luke, chapter 16, verses 1-15, the Bible relates another regarding this practice. It is called "The Parable of the Shrewd Steward." In this story, the manager was discovered engaging in bad management by his superior and was soon to be laid off. Before his last day of work, the manager evaluated his circumstances before deciding to gain "leverage" on other people. He was still in the position or had the authority to liaise with the business associates. He used his current capacity to build good relations with his business associates while he could. He was called 'shrewd" and was commended even by his superior!

In today's world, it is called 'survival of the fittest." It is stated in verse 8 that "people of this world are shrewder in dealing with their own kind than the people of light;" meaning, that man will look out for himself to survive. It is the innate nature of man. But the people of light are different. They are to "use worldly wealth to gain friends… that take you into eternal dwellings." The virtue of wisdom exists for both types of people here but the focus is different. The worldly person will use his wisdom to survive for the now whereas the people of light will use that same wisdom for the future – eternity.

So, how you handle these "fringe benefits" or "favors" reflect your wisdom on your focus. Using what you are given wisely impacts you and others for life and beyond. Be not myopic by looking at the NOW but look further. That is called "planning". The saying goes, "If you fail to plan, you plan to fail."

Lesson: These so-called "unethical" practices have been in existence since time immortal; it is the HOW they are handled with WHAT focus in mind that is more important than the WHAT is received and WHY.

How to overcome unethical practices in Office Politics
People in authority or in some position in the company will encounter such practices; they are really unavoidable. Do a self-check if you are practicing for the NOW or for THEN (future). Does the practice benefit only you to gratify yourself or are you truly helping another in need without dire consequences to the company and others around you?
If you are unsure of the practice, consult your superior, or a third party who is not involved, for a second and unbiased opinion before you make the decision. People of light would pray for God's leading and intervention, for all things will work out well as they entrust themselves to God's wisdom. (Romans 8:28)

Personal note: These practices are not all bad, but as we know, too much of something often leads to dire consequences. These practices can be a good form of appreciation expressed by those who required a helping hand, but should not be made a habit or even worse, a demand. That is when you would have incurred the "wrath" of your colleagues.

c. Scenario 3 – Favoritism
Romans 2:11 – For God does not show favoritism

Nobody likes to be on the sidelines, because if you are, you are only an observer. You are not the active participant or recipient of the excitement happening on the field. That's where the attention is. That's where the adrenalin flow is the greatest.
Thus, it is frustrating for those on the outside looking in, even in the office. To see others enjoying the favor of the superiors is very demoralizing. You feel insignificant and slighted with self-esteem going lower than the samba bar. How is it that others are preferred over you? What do they have that you don't? What did they do that you didn't?

Sometimes you feel there is no answer to your questions.
The Bible records similar situations where favoritism is concerned. Let's look at it from two points of view: The employee and the employer or the worker and the one in authority.

First, the employee's outlook: In the book of Matthew chapter 20, verse 20 to verse 28, a determined mother decided to make a bold request to position her sons at the very top.

James and John are brothers who have been following Jesus for some time, along with 10 others. They have been at Jesus' side since He called them to join Him in his "adventures." So, Jesus can be considered these guys' leader or superior. Then one day, James and John's mother came to Jesus and asked Him to grant both her sons the seats of honor, one at Jesus' left and the other at Jesus' right, when Jesus is established in His reign. That is outright requested favoritism ! Within each of us, we desire to be the boss' "right-hand man," his trusted aid, his confidante, his favored one. It is an excellent position to be in besides the top post, because it is the most secure in a work environment.

Jesus addressed the boys directly in this matter, for He knew it was really their desire as much as it was their mother's. As their leader and authority, Jesus knew their capabilities, their characters and their ambitions. However, it is not just one person's say to appoint another into a high position even if he is in authority. There may be other superiors to whom a leader is accountable. Things at the office usually happen for the overall good of the office. There is always a board of trustees guarding over the welfare of the company to whom every employee is accountable to on his or her words, actions or productivity.

Another group of employees found in this scenario are those on the sidelines. When they heard about the bold request or the expressed desire of the brothers, they were indignant! How dare the brothers openly express their desire to be favored! It was actually in everyone's heart but no one had expressed it openly. Employees tend to harbor such ambition, which is not wrong, but their related skills, knowledge and capabilities need to be proven before they are recognized for any promotions. One has to keep alert to the opportunities to make such a move.

Next, the employer's viewpoint: Luke 14:7-11
However the employee may think that he deserves the coveted position more than anyone else, the employer or his superior may hold a different viewpoint or agenda. In the book of Luke, chapter 14 tells of Jesus' observation of the invited guests to a social event. The guests tend to pick the places of honor at the table upon arrival to the function, but Jesus advises otherwise, giving His reason. There may be another guest who is more important or distinguished than you and you might have just chosen the seat reserved for him. You will be embarrassed when you are asked to vacate the seat, and as there probably will be no good seats left by that time, you will move to one of the worst seats in the place. That would be a real embarrassment. Similarly, in the office, the superior may have in mind someone else for a coveted position or task, and the employee has only to perform his best to exhibit his capabilities and potential to be invited to that honor. Superiors are usually set in place because they have a certain ability to identify the employees' or company's strengths or potential for the general welfare of the company.

Lesson: The walls have ears and eyes. The superiors are in the know. They are set in place to identify the right candidate(s) who can contribute positively or significantly to the welfare of the company. They may assign tasks to these potential candidates to confirm their capabilities while others on the sidelines may view this as favoritism.

How to overcome favoritism in Office Politics
Nothing an employee does or says is really hidden. It is better to eat humble pie and take every opportunity to give your best to shine or exhibit your capabilities so that you will be identified for the coveted position. If a company really believes that its employees are its greatest assets, then those in authority will certainly be on the lookout for genuine employees who have what it takes to move the company to another notch in business.

d. Scenario 4 – Malicious Gossip
1 Peter 2:1 – Therefore, rid yourselves of all malice and all deceit, hypocrisy, envy and slander of every kind.

Gossips are very common in the office environment where people act out of spite. It could be the result of uncontrolled restraints of a person who exaggerates to get more attention or to make his input on the matter more interesting, thus sowing seeds of discord in the office although much of what is said is untrue.

The Bible also reveals this common scenario where a group of people was trying to complete a task but they were discouraged and distracted in their task as their accusers spread malicious gossip about their intention.

For those interested in the biblical context, the book of Ezra, chapters 4 to 6 record how a certain group of people had asked the king's permission to rebuild the temple of God in Jerusalem. When another group of people was unhappy over the task that was in progress, they set out to discourage the workers by instilling fear through bad advice and discouragement. When a change of kings took place, the opposition accused this group of builders of disrespecting the new king with its rebellious nature as from days of old, thus causing a 'stop work" gag order by the new king.

However, the builders did not give up or let themselves be discouraged. They waited for the right opportunity to bring the issue up before the right authority – the next king, and clarified the matter humbly.

The new king, in his wisdom and fairness, confirmed that these builders had received permission from the first king to rebuild the temple, and he allowed the work to be carried on to completion.

Lesson: There will be people who are unhappy over your good progress or performance and may attempt to derail you from your assigned task or responsibilities through gossip and accusations. Sometimes, it pays to 'stop work" for the moment, especially when the situation is too hot to handle immediately. Just like a hot potato, you need to let it cool before picking it up.

The truth shall always surface as the right opportunity arises for you to make your stand and state your case to the relevant authority, and justice shall prevail.

How to overcome gossip and accusations in Office Politics

It pays to be patient. Patience is a virtue. If you are in this situation, you may want to follow the 'stop work" order that is thrown at you; not that you are "guilty" of its baseless accusations or gossips, but no amount of explanation will be heard in your favor, when the accusers have done quite a good job at smearing your name and reputation.

Be patient for the right time to explain yourself or your situation, if you have acted righteously or in accordance with the truth or instructions. Sometimes when the situation is too hot to handle and we try to pacify or "douse the flames," there will be more heat and smoke to cloud everyone's sense of justice. Your attempts to explain may be deemed as trying to justify why you are in the wrong. When you learn to speak at the opportune time, you will be heard clearly and favorably.

38

God knows and sees all. The book of Proverbs chapter 15, verse 3 says, "The eyes of the Lord are everywhere, keeping watch on the wicked and the good." God is God of the earth and the heavens; He will pave the way for you to find favor with the authority and clear your name. The book of Psalms, chapter 1clearly states that "the Lord watches over the way of the righteous but the way of the wicked will perish." If you trust in God, who made the heavens and the earth, and created you, you need not worry or fear anything or anyone, for He will put everything right for you in His own time.

e. Scenario 5 – The Trump Card

1 Corinthians 10:24 – No one should seek his own good but the good of others.

Many employees have tried this tactic to add mileage to their career path, especially when they are ambitious and feel they are "quite" indispensable. They know that they are assets to the company and they try to force the superior's arm to their favor. Their threats to resign unless their conditions are met can work out well or be disastrous for them. It is a risk they are taking, and they need to be wise with these kinds of calculated risks.

The Bible speaks of a similar character known as Judas Iscariot, who had been following Jesus for about 3 years with others. Judas considered himself to be an "important worker" as he holds the position of group treasurer, in charge of the group's moneybag. Although he dipped into the group's finances at times for his personal use, greed got the better of him in due time. He played his trump card. He had information and access to his leader's whereabouts and happenings. He could make a profit with this information, so he set about looking for the right buyer. In the book of Matthew, chapter 26, verses 14-16, he found willing buyers who would pay for the information and assistance he could offer them towards gaining an upper hand over a matter. Judas calculated the risk of the situation. He reasoned, "Why *not gain mileage with the information or privileges I hold and make them work to my benefit?*" He threw out his trump card, collected his dues and entered into a contract, but in the end, he lost out and lost badly, to the extent of losing his life. (Matthew 27:1-5)

Lesson: A trump card is something you have or hold that is private to you. It can work well for you if you handle it carefully and wisely. It may backfire on you if you do not check out all the possibilities and loopholes. It is a gamble using a trump card, because life is an event of probabilities. There are 2 sides to every coin.

How to overcome misusing the Trump Card in Office Politics
You might be in a certain position in the office where you are privileged to have access to certain people or important information, which should be kept, private and confidential. You might think that you are "indispensable" to the company; a definite asset, a valued employee - an important piece in the structure. Don't flatter yourself.

No matter how important you think you are or how valuable an asset to the company, the truth of the matter is, no one is indispensable. Unless you are the Board Chairman or the company owner, you do not know ALL about the inside dealings or information pertaining to the company; thus, your trump card is not worth what you think it may be.

The trump card is best used when it is used subtly and with humility, which never hurts anyone, no matter how much you exercise it. This way, you don't get publicly embarrassed when the deal doesn't go through.

f. Scenario 6 – Manipulation

Matthew 6:19 – Do not store for yourselves treasures on earth, where moth and rust destroy, and where thieves break in and steal.

Let's refer again to the Parable of the Shrewd Steward in the New Testament in the book of Luke, chapter 16 from verses 1-15.

Here we have a manager who manipulated his position to gain mileage for himself while he could, as the opportunity presented itself. He was shrewd as he thought about his future and how he could secure it as he moves on in life.

He exercised manipulation on what was not really his, as he gave "discounts" to others owing the company, to gain himself some benefits. That is really the essence of manipulation. You make use of others, or even their belongings and properties, to gain mileage for yourself.

Although it is a good virtue to be alert to opportunities and to seize it while it is day, it is unethical to take other's belongings to benefit self, especially without the consent of the owner. Similarly, it is not right if manipulation is done on people without their consent. The Bible teaches us to be shrewd to the situation; that is, to keep alert to the changes occurring around us so that we can adjust wisely to survive well in this world, for continuity sake in righteousness, not through manipulation.

Lesson: Manipulation is quite devious as it represents itself as harmless but it does put on a deceiving front, which is not how one should live his or her life. Manipulation can pull your life or reputation down when the situation goes awry, and it is hard to rebuild the trust you lose. It is possible for one to make use of manipulation. The question is, which kind? The Bible states in the book of Luke chapter 16, verse 9, that one can "use worldly wealth to gain friends for yourself, so that when it is gone, you will be welcomed into eternal dwellings."

How to overcome Manipulation in Office Politics

Manipulation should be applied on things, not people. Things can be used to bring on the good effect on people, not to harm or to discredit people. Manipulate to bless, not to hurt or destroy. Make use of things or objects or possessions to benefit, such as how we would use the car to take us wherever we want to go, or money to bring joy and ease to others rather than for self; but in the end, the joy and benefit return to you.

Each person is of value and deserves the proper respect as part of the human race; none should be manipulated. Every person should be blessed. If we are so concerned about the animals or plants (green the earth!), we should be concerned for another human – our same kind!

It is not necessary to outdo one another in the office. There is no need for manipulation at the office, as each one is assigned his or her portion. Isn't that the reason you were hired into the organization? Employees in a company are like the cogs of the machine; each one functions as designated and the whole machine runs smoothly. If manipulation is prevalent, the "cogs" will be stuck or confused, distracted from their proper functioning and that will be detrimental to the welfare of the organization. Companies are split or closed down because of manipulation within, with the parties wanting to gain control or power in the organization. The ones who suffer most will be the employees.

The Bible states in the book of Philippians chapter 4, verse 11, to be "content whatever the circumstances." It is learning that one needs to undergo, for your portion in life is in God's hands. The parable of the Rich Fool in the book of Luke chapter 12, verses 13-21, mentions how a rich man plans (or manipulates) the future with what he has to get more but in the end, died suddenly, because as mortal man, one cannot determine how and when your life ends. Verse 15 in Luke chapter 12 states, a "man's life does not consist in the abundance of his possession," which is basically greed, underpinning manipulation.

Many of us waste our time and effort manipulating others instead of being more productive or fruitful according to our abilities. It is sufficient to be as productive as you can for that is your makeup; that is your 100%.

g. Scenario 7 – Scratching Each Other's Back

Hebrews 13:6 – And do not forget to do good and to share with others, for with such sacrifices God is pleased.

Watching out for one another to benefit each other is a common display of office politics where the involved parties are comfortable with each other to have gained trust in one another. When used well, this practice can bring tremendous results benefitting each other.

Just like the Bible record of how the people of the world in ancient times worked together to build a tower that could reach the heavens (Old Testament book of Genesis, chapter 11 verses 1-4). They had a common goal and understanding. They were ambitious. They made plans for their future and were to be satisfied with "making a name for themselves."

It is really quite amazing what man can do and achieve when he puts his mind to it; all the more when there are two or more of them like-minded. Thus, we have seen the rapid growth of the Industrial Revolution, and now the astounding developments from the Technology Era.

But it is not always possible to depend on Man alone, for Man is finite with weaknesses. He may betray his fellow mates when tempted or motivated by greed. His priorities may change and those changes may not include his faithful and long-trusting partners. You might find yourself "played out" in the game, so to speak.

So, while it looks like a good arrangement for the involved parties to exercise this practice, it is not sustainable for the long run. Even in the Bible record, the men were discarded. Their priorities and manners changed, and they were scattered. Misunderstandings may arise and mistrust is developed. Paths diverge.

Lesson: Although it is necessary to work together, it is foolish to trust another 100%. Even Jesus did not trust man, for He knew what is in a man. If you need to trust someone, try Jesus. He said in the book of John chapter 14, verse 1: "Do not let your hearts be troubled. Trust in God, trust also in Me" for "never will I leave you or forsake you" (Hebrews 13:5).

How to overcome Scratching Each Other's Back in Office Politics
Always act professionally. Remember that you got the job based on YOUR own merits, and that should be enough to keep you there. You may have to work with others and you can do your part responsibly and professionally without being too attached or involved, so that any success due you will be credited to you. Your work and work ethics are really quite clear for others to see, although you think you have covered your tracks. So, better to keep an open front where you can continue as you are, making an honest living than to waste your time and effort on putting on layer after layer of makeup to cover any flaws or blemishes. Just as too much makeup is not healthy for the skin and body, especially in the long run, so is back-scratching to the soul.

h. Scenario 8 – Backstabbing

1 Peter 3:8 – "Finally, all of you, live in harmony with one another; be sympathetic, love as brothers, be compassionate and humble."

Backstabbing is a malicious form of office politics as the term implies. It is a vicious attack on someone who is unaware of the harm or danger he or she is in. A malicious employee who wishes to climb up the ladder may devise means and ways to reach his goal through manipulation or harassment; the latter being more aggressive and with pre-planned intent to "wipe out" any person hindering his purpose or progress. A colleague may set up a situation in which untruths may be spread in order to cause disrepute to the competition. The Bible records many instances where different groups of people back-stab others to get forward, which result in many "casualties" and victims.

One particular instance is Joseph who was his father's blue-eyed boy amongst his eleven brothers. Although he was very straightforward his manners and speech, which some may have misinterpreted as arrogance, he was betrayed by his own brothers, who devised ill plans to befall the young man, causing him to be separated from his father and family at a young age. This incident is recorded in the Old Testament's first book, Genesis, in chapter 37. This goes to show what kind of nature humans have as they can devise ill on their own kind, much more on their own family member, their own flesh and blood! But God has a unique way of working through people whom He created, for He knows our shortcomings. **The situation for Joseph ended well** when he rose to be a very prominent man in a foreign land and forgave his brothers for the harm they had intended on him in the past. That is the great virtue of a mature and righteous man who holds no wrong against another who did wrong to him. God blessed him for that virtue!

Lesson: There are bound to be victims and casualties in backstabbing, and it should not be undertaken as all men are created equal. Just as the world is round, there is a cause and effect, which will befall the backstabber. Since the harm will come around to you, if you are the initiator, don't venture into it in the first place.

How to overcome back-stabbing in office politics
If you are angry with another in the office, and wish some form of revenge, think again. The Bible states, "Vengeance is mine, says the Lord" in the Old Testament book of Deuteronomy chapter 32, verse 35, and twice in the New Testament, in the books of Romans (chapter 12, verse 19) and Hebrews (chapter 10, verse 30). And if God takes the time to repeat His words, He must really be serious about that issue!

So, no matter how wronged we think we have had it, if you fear God, He will step out for you as He did for Joseph and Jesus and for all of whom He loves.

But what if the role is reversed? What if you think you have been betrayed, what are you to do about it? Do you retaliate with confrontation or vengeance (which has been mentioned just before)? Currently, there is a trendy jewelry piece with the letters "WWJD" amongst youth, which has spread to adults and children too. Its initials stand for "What Would Jesus Do." It is a reminder for those who believe and trust in God and Jesus, that we should do what Jesus would have done in that same situation if He had gone through it, as He was a man just like each of us, having experienced what man experiences today.

So, would Jesus understand your feelings if you have been a victim of betrayal? Yes, indeed He would have understood. The Bible recorded many times how He was backstabbed and betrayed by those closest to Him. He was sneered at by His own kind, rejected by His own people, unaccepted by His own earthly siblings, and the list goes on. Yes, Jesus has experienced it all as a man, and would be able to understand how a man feels when he undergoes a difficult situation.

Jesus did what Joseph did in days of old. They both did what God had planned for them to do, even when they underwent trying times. The focal point is really not that point in time when you are backstabbed, but the end result. Truly, the final result is what is referred to here. Joseph and Jesus went through horrible times being betrayed. While Joseph came out well in the end and made up with his "wrong-doers", Jesus was crucified. But the very end result for Jesus is not His crucifixion but His resurrection (John chapter 11 verse 35), and His coming again to judge and reign! (Please refer to the book of Revelation)

There is always closure to every situation; it is a matter of the right time. Are you patient enough to wait for your grand "deliverance", or do you take matters into your own hands, and maybe make matters worse? The choice is yours.

i. Scenario 9 – Hypocrisy

{Matthew 5:37 – Simply let your "Yes" be "Yes" and your "No", "No"}

Deception is the main focal point in hypocrisy. When one colleague is identified as a hypocrite, one must keep the distance and always be alert to the hypocrite's ways and words, for that character is truly a "wolf in sheep's clothing". The Bible warns of such persons who come in disguise, to mingle with the unsuspecting crowd as he is "dressed" like one of them, but with intentions to 'steal, kill and destroy."

Jesus mentioned it in the New Testament book of John, chapter 10, where the wolf comes to kill, steal and destroy. Anyone who does not enter the sheep pen through the sheep gate is a thief and a robber. His intentions are bad if he does not go about his business or life in the right or acceptable manner. He is likened to the wolf, which wants to attack the sheep and scatter them. Hypocrisy in the office is the same. Its bottom line is to destroy others with untruth and deception. It is dangerous.

Referring to those people building a temple again in the book of Ezra chapter 4, another group was seemingly kind to offer their help in the building but was rejected because the builders saw through them. The rejected were hypocrites and their true wicked intentions surfaced as they turned around to spread lies and bad rumors about the builders, causing the latter much hardship in their task.

Daniel, an official **in the Babylonian** kingdom, experienced no less in hypocritical situations. Although he was upright in his ways and handled his responsibilities with distinction, he was often the subject of ridicule and envy, to the extent that hypocrisy was acted against him. His "colleagues" turned against him, as mentioned in the Old Testament, in the book of Daniel (chapter 6, verse 4), where time and again, Daniel was wrongfully accused. Instead of working together in harmony, Daniel's colleagues were worried about their own positions, although they had been awarded the status and authority as Daniel. Insecurity and envy can cause hypocrisy to surface.

Jesus taught his disciples to be alert to hypocrisy in the New Testament book of Matthew, chapter 6, verse 6, **where many learned people instructed others in how to live and behave,** but they themselves did not practice what they taught. That is the essence of hypocrisy – not walking the talk; and it stems from insincerity in a person who has ulterior motives or a hidden personal agenda.

Lesson: Hypocrisy changes a person's life, and once changed, it is difficult to regain the original state of being, which is reflective of how one's life would be if marred by hypocrisy. There is really no fairy tale, happy ending with those who practice hypocrisy, as seen from life's examples and the biblical examples.

How to overcome Hypocrisy in office politics
Stay true to yourself. You have earned the right to be in the office at your position. Knowing that hypocrisy brings more damage than good, it is best to be alert to those who practice hypocrisy and avoid them. You have better things to do than to be engaged with such people and unbeneficial works. You should make wise use of your time in the office, building up your portfolio for promotion and recognition from the company than to be involved in hypocrisy. That will also make you more marketable outside the office as you build up your good and credible reputation in the market.

It is better to climb up the ladder through honest means than through hypocrisy. It is hard to get out of hypocrisy once you are embroiled in it, and you might not be even aware of your involvement until you are seriously involved.

A bad reputation spreads like wildfire. If your reputation of being duplicitous is made public, your reputation will be discredited in the marketplace, causing difficulties for you to move in that circle of business. Hence, it is better not to get started in hypocrisy in the first place.

j. Scenario 10 – Whistle-Blowing

Matthew 5:37 – Simply let your "Yes" be "Yes" and your "No", "No".

Whistle blowing can have consequences - usually bad ones, although good outcomes are possible as in saving a life or preventing a situation from turning gangrenous. Sometimes it is needful to "whistle-blow" to prevent further damage, because the party involved may not be brave enough to voice out and someone else has to take the initiative. The whistle-blower may get into trouble if the situation is not amicably resolved, as the involved party may feel betrayed and land himself in trouble.

An instance in the Bible where such an incident occurred can be found in the book of Matthew chapter 18, verses 23 to 34. It is the parable of the unmerciful servant, where this employee owed the employer money. When the time came for repayment, the employee could not settle his outstanding amount. The employer intended to send him off to jail until he paid his debt. He begged for mercy and out of compassion, was granted a cancellation of his debts. But he went out and found another fellow employee who owed him a smaller sum and demanded repayment, which the fellow employee could not repay. In a fit of anger, he sent his fellow employee to jail. Other employees saw the treatment he gave to his colleague and they went to report the incident to the employer who clearly was annoyed with the employee. The employer took the unmerciful employee to task by sending him to jail, as per his original punishment.

Hence, it was other employees who blew the whistle on the unmerciful employee who did not practice the good that was bestowed on him.

Lesson: This is the good kind of whistle blowing by those who upheld good moral principles. Everyone is an employee, but some have more problems than others. Each should be given a pinch of compassion and some leeway in times of difficulty. Everyone should be on the alert to their surroundings. If the weak are unable to defend themselves, then the stronger ones should step in to assist. That is the purpose of humankind, not to lord over others but to ensure fair treatment to the needy.

How to overcome Whistle Blowing in office politics

In the office, every employee needs to be alert to his or her environment. You cannot be always on the sidelines or hide away under your shell as in your room or cubicle. Being a part of the company, you owe it to the organization, your colleagues, and to yourself to stand up on moral issues. You need to stand up for the weak and needy in their defense, if you are able. Making excuses to avoid a political situation in the office does not always benefit you; there will be times when you need assistance from others. There are many fables and real stories where "one good deed returns another." Good deeds are like boomerangs; they come back to you.

But there is another kind of whistle blowing that is filled with bad intention. It is meant to degrade the involved party or to unmercifully expose his faults. It can land the victim in trouble. When you want to blow the whistle on someone at work, consider compassion. What is your real intention? Is it really for justice or for self? Even if it is for justice, is there room in your heart for compassion, like the employer to the employee in the above parable. Everyone deserves a second chance. If you can give your colleague a second chance, you won't have to inform on him.

SUCCESSFUL PROFILES – SURVIVORS OF OFFICE POLITICS (7)

Famous Men & Women

Surely there are many successful businessmen and businesswomen out there in the marketplace today who have dealt successfully with office politics. Many would be simple employees, while others could be employers or entrepreneurs holding esteemed positions of authority and power in some high-profile organization.

How did these successful people succeed with office politics? By standing on the principles of integrity, forthrightness, trustworthiness and honor, these people tasted success.

a. Mother Teresa

"By blood, I am Albanian; by citizenship, an Indian. By faith, I am a Catholic nun. As to my calling, I belong to the world. As to my heart, I belong entirely to the Heart of Jesus"

The declaration of Mother Teresa is so simple, yet true and touching. One can feel her sincerity oozing out from those simple words she used to define herself. Though petite, she was strong in other ways. Mother Teresa did not falter in her God-given mission and went about doing her task as assigned by the Divine. She was just a simple woman who was sent off to a huge mission. It is mind-boggling to even think how Mother Teresa coped, much less started and ended her task.

She went to the poorest of the poor in Calcutta, India, something not many of us would even think of. She had a mission and she went about it quietly doing what she could without calling for attention or recognition.

Mother Teresa experienced pain and hardship even at a young age when her father died suddenly, leaving her family in deep poverty. Her mother was her greatest influence while she grew, loving but firm, Mother Teresa caught on her mother's characteristics to shape her own character and vocation. Mother Teresa became a missionary after arriving in India in 1929 to serve in Calcutta.

She became committed to her divine calling to the Sisters of Loreto, and lived her life selflessly with a natural talent or capacity for good organization. She was noted for her generous character, her courage and her capacity for hard work.

Although she received a higher calling or task to care for the poorest of the poor on September 10, 1946, while in a train traveling from Calcutta to Darjeeling, Mother Teresa encountered many setbacks and lack of support for about 2 years before she could establish a religious community called Missionaries of Charity for that purpose. ***This is another veil of office politics where superiors would be the key players in discouraging underlings from doing what*** *subordinates think was right. It is usually a case of a "just take orders from me" attitude from superiors who may feel threatened by a subordinate's creativity or capability. Hence, a subordinate's suggestions are usually not favorable to the superior, who plays office politics to safeguard his own position.* With Mother Teresa, she was undeterred in her desire, as she knew her calling was from a greater authority – God. She took the first step out of the convent to the streets of the poorest on August 17, 1948, in a blue-bordered white sari.

As she visited the slums for the first time, she saw poor families in great need, and tended to them as best as she could, washing the children's sores, caring for a sick old man on the roadside and nursing a dying woman of TB and malnutrition. She went about her task alone for the *"unwanted, unloved and uncared for"* for a few months before her ex-students joined her quest one after another.

When her work drew much positive public and foreign attention, the Archdiocese of Calcutta recognized her organization. *Office politics can also come in disguised forms; quick in changing its tune is one of its characteristics when success or positive output is favored and great support is now thrown at the "prodigal" who has done well.*

Mother Teresa continued to send out workers into other needy areas of India. Soon, her work made an impact on almost every country with their organization's presence, including Cuba, Albania and the former Soviet Union. Mother Teresa openly shared her lifestyle and knowledge humbly to all who would be inspired by her. She accepted people of different nationalities and faiths with the same loving and giving spirit. She listened to the requests of people around her as they feedback on their needs. She made effort to give others what they needed.

Her great works brought much public attention until she was awarded with numerous accolades from the Indian Padmashri Award in 1962 to the famous Nobel Peace Prize in 1979. She was always humble when receiving any award, making it clear that she did not receive it for herself. *A true worker does not seek rewards for self, which is unlike those in office politicking.*

The world may view Mother Teresa's life as most honorable as she sacrificed her own comforts to serve the poorest and the most needy with love, joy and dignity. *But others may sneer at her foolishness to give up her own comfort to care for others. There are always different sides when one is on a task. Office politicking always has its supporters on both sides. Mother Teresa did not bother about which side had more supporters for her cause. She only drew closer to her one source of strength – her God. He was her guiding light which hid all the shadows and kept her focused on her divine calling. This led Mother Teresa to deeper experiences and character development.*

Mother Teresa trudged on with her responsibilities despite severe poor health during her final years on earth. She established 610 foundations with about 4,000 members worldwide. She was wise to appoint a successor to continue the work she started at an appropriate time before spending her final weeks in Calcutta, still receiving people and giving final instructions or teachings.

Mother Teresa exhibited a rock-solid faith, a sure hope and selfless charity.

It is certainly not easy to kick-start something which you have in mind or feel very passionate about. Hiccups and obstacles will surface and may even stubbornly persist to test your determination and capability to overcome. *Mother Teresa knew her calling well and stood her ground, waiting for the right moment to start on her mission. This is the most likely scenario when one works in an office environment, with a superior (or superiors). Patience must be acquired. Even with approvals, other obstacles may present themselves at various points of your work journey, through no fault or error of your own.*

What should your response be? Mother Teresa's response was to keep focused on her mission and she went about it step by step, going the way alone before others came on board. She did not give up through disappointments or setbacks. The work environment may not have been the most favorable, as Mother Teresa found out, but she worked her way through gently and slowly, picking up the pieces along the way, touching one at a time. The work place can be improved if one adopts Mother Teresa's way of working and attitude.

Mother Teresa became a legend after she died; most of us would want to leave a legacy when our time on earth is done, too.

b. Mao Tse-tung

Mao Tse-tung, who in 1949 established the People's Republic of China, is considered a great theorist in Marxism with Vladimir, Lenin and Karl Marx. Mao founded the Communist party in China, where he was born in 1893. Although he was in constant conflict with his father during his childhood, Mao learned to confront the strictness exhibited by his father.

When Sun Yat-sen launched his attack overture on the now defunct Ch"ing dynasty in 1911, Mao was in Chang-sha province confronting the political changes that were rapidly sweeping the nation with a new cultural movement. He served a short stint in the nation's republican army before engaging himself in independent study at the provincial library, graduating from Hunan's First Normal School in 1918.

In Peking, Mao was too poor to continue his studies in the University and did not master any foreign languages.. Although he did not rub shoulders with cosmopolitan intellects at the Chinese university, he did interact with Chinese radical intellectuals who were prominent in the nation's Communist party. He was self-supporting while engaging in radical political activity when he went back to Hunan in 1919. He organized radical groups on political activities while churning out a political review.

His wife, Yang K"ai-hui, whom he married in 1920, was later executed by the Chinese Nationalists in 1930. After that, Mao married twice.

Mao became one of the founding members of the Chinese Communist party in 1921. He led the Hunan branch in working along the Kuomintang while engaging in labor and party organizations, propaganda and the Peasant Movement. But when Chiang Kai-shek took over the Kuomintang leadership in 1927, after Sun Yat-sen's death, Mao fled to the suburbs when Chiang went on a purging spree of Communists. Mao teamed up with a guerrilla army to fuse Communism with guerilla force, which enjoyed peasant support to establish Mao as CCP leader. By the group's strong military power, Mao managed to establish a Chinese Soviet in Juichin instead of following the Russian-controlled CCP.

Although Mao encountered resistance from the Nationalist government, he managed to end the Russian leadership in Kweichow when his forces marched to Shensi in 1935 to establish the party's new HQ at Yen-an.

The Japanese invasion in 1937 forced Kuomintang and CCP to cooperate again, which gave Mao the opportunity to rise as the nation's leader, establishing his own self as a Marxist thinker and military theorist. Mao wrote many essays, which formed the basis of his party's control over the nation's cultural affairs. Mao's confidence in his ruling theories and guerilla strategies gave rise to the huge increase in the party's membership from 40,000 in 1937 to 1,200,000 in 1945.

Mao's Communist Party parted ways with the Nationalists at the end of WWII although the U.S. made efforts to unite the two, only to see the eruption of civil wars, which led to Kuomintang's defeat. Hence, Mao formed the new government under the banner of People's Republic of China in 1949, controlling the whole of main land China.

After Mao failed to establish good relations with the U.S., he leaned China towards the USSR, and a close alliance was formed. China became more hostile towards the U.S. through the Korean War and Mao's international fame was established after Joseph Stalin, Soviet leader, died in 1953.

Mao exhibited a unique leadership trait where he committed to the struggle of the commoners or, peasantry, under the banner of socialism. Mao exhibited dissatisfaction over the slow development and forsaken countryside revolutionary momentum as CCP members began to take on an affluent air and lifestyle. He boldly kick-started a few unusual initiatives where he strongly encouraged intellectuals to give constructive criticism with regard to the party's stewardship. ***Here, we pause to ponder over the real motives of such frustration. Many ambitious*** *subordinates are quick to grab any opportunity that they see could be a stepping stone for their career. Once a "good cause" was formulated, the ambitious employee would put in effort to gain supporters to push forth his personal goals through the "good cause" presented. He is well aware that numbers mean power. The larger the quantum, the greater the power harnessed for pushing forward his personal agenda. It is called the "people's power" when in reality, the underpinning factor is a personal agenda to power and self-glory.*

As the saying goes, when the hornet's nest is stirred, trouble follows. Mao's new and different initiative opened to office politicking where many of his compatriots were divided. Some critiqued the initiative, while others seized the opportunity to voice their opinions, perhaps to further their own political agendas.

These sudden initiatives administered by Mao did not bode well with many of his compatriots who moved in to take him down. They did eventually, as confusion in the administration arose and the adverse weather caused severe crop shortfalls, leading to high food shortages; these were attributed to Mao's poor management. As a consequence, Mao lost his influence and position in the CCP. ***When one uses the "trump card" unwisely in an office politicking situation, its consequences can be adverse. One needs to be alert and thoroughly informed before putting out a trump card in office politics.***

But Mao was determined to rise from the dust again, as one would when he is ambitious in any office politicking. Through the strong support of his wife, who orchestrated the Cultural Revolution in 1966-1969, Mao took on the right platform for establishing his ideological struggle through public opinions and national debates, exhibiting his skills in tactics maneuvering. He had his ideologies carried off by press and students who were his best supporters. *If one were to succeed in office politicking, there must be a strong and big support behind, regardless if the cause is right or otherwise. Mao manipulated his political way very well this time round* as he accepted the military support in return of Lin Piao as successor due to increasing tensions and possible chaos. But as luck would have it, Lin died in 1971 only to have Mao re-establish his control of China.

The Cultural Revolution was just one of Mao's main thrusts in his political ambition. Actually, world politics is just a bigger version of office politics. The former is on a bigger scale than the latter but the players are about the same - ambitious people who vied for power and prestige through working others to form their support and power. Hence, Mao's Cultural Revolution did move the way its leader set it up. The Chinese masses were "induced" on their right and privilege to revolt and criticize those in power or authority. They were influenced to take an active role in making decisions for the nation's welfare, which were recorded in Mao's little red book that has been infamously handed to the masses. *Mao orchestrated all these in his political ambition. But the people's eyes and minds were veiled to the truth behind the scenes.* Hence, Mao was regarded with ecstatic adulation.

Mao tried to move up the ladder to foreign circles, as he would in any office environment, where one would gain a foothold in the department before moving on to the upper management portfolio. Mao tried to link up with the U.S., which he viewed as one of the world superpowers at that time (besides the USSR) and met up with Richard Nixon in 1972 in Peking. Mao labeled China as an underdeveloped or Third World nation of which he was not too favorable. *He wanted to put China on a par with the superpowers; that is precisely the obvious step taken by those who are in office politicking. It is never sufficient to be the department head. One must aim higher and, perhaps, be accepted into the Board of Directors.*

As there are ups and downs with office politics, so it is in the political world. With Mao's death in 1976, and the arrest of his wife and associates, moderates group led by Teng Hsio-P 'ing overthrew Mao's successor. The previous Cultural Revolution excesses were criticized while praises heaped on Mao's earlier leadership style where the 1982 Constitution declared that progress and economic cooperation are more important elements in building up a nation than class struggle. Hence, all personality cults were banned and Mao's beliefs were also not spared, with many of his statues being removed throughout China.

When one falls from grace in any office environment, his reputation is smeared through the mud. Thankfully for Mao, he did not have to see it in his lifetime. No one can last forever in an office politics or world politics situation, and Mao was proof, no matter how strong he was. Hence, a different viewpoint on Mao arose when in 1989, a Central Advisory Commission member declared in the Guangming Daily newspaper that "Mao was a great man who embodied the calamities of the Chinese people, but in his later years he made big mistakes over a long period, and the result was great disaster for the people and the country. He created a historical tragedy."

Besides the Han and Ming dynasties, Mao Tse-tung was the third leader of peasant birth who rose to rule the whole of China in his lifetime. His most impressive achievements include uniting China by destroying the Nationalists and setting up the People's Republic based on a leadership style that is socially revolutionizing in the whole of human history.

This new class of revolution involved the land and property collectivization, landlord class elimination, urban bourgeoisie weakening and peasant cum industrial workers" status elevation.

Mao Tse-tung was regarded by many as a great leader who did not forget his roots, and it was clearly exhibited throughout his leadership that his intention was to raise the standard of living for the peasants with appropriate initiatives to redistribute wealth to the peasants who heavily populated the nation. The struggles of Mao did not keep him down or out as he continued unwaveringly in his quest, *(as one would in an office environment to wait for the right opportunity before making his strike)*, waited for the right time and opportunity to field his ideology again, garnering support from the right groups to convey his heart's passion *(which resembles the same steps that an office political advocator would take on)*. Whether in office politics or world politics, a deep passion is great motivation to move to greater heights no matter how long the course may take or what struggles come along the way. Results will be observed if one does not give up on your vision when sustained by the passion. *The question is, "would you be listening to your conscience?"*

c. Bill Gates

Every businessman or woman knows Bill Gates, if not personally, at least by name and his amazing business feats, being one of the world's most influential business personalities. As cofounder of the world's most notable computer software, Microsoft, Bill Gates has been considered the world's richest man for the past few years.

Although Bill Gates started his junior year at Harvard University, he soon dropped out to start his business venture with Paul Allen to establish the renowned Microsoft Corporation software company in 1975. Its company Mission Statement is "*to enable people and businesses throughout the world to realize their full potential."*

Microsoft became an instant success commercially with its versatile MS-DOS operating system, along with Gates' proactive measures against software piracy. Gates retired from the CEO position in 2008.

Bill Gates Criticism
With his acclaimed success, abundant criticisms also abound as Gates exercised his business philosophy ambitiously and aggressively, resulting in many legal battles against software piracy. *This is really office politics on a wider scale, not as big as world politics but definitely beyond the walls of one workplace. It is office politics in the business arena. With talent and creativity, one can use a trump card to maneuver the situation to his favor.* Bill Gates was creative and talented to chart the path for his company's success. His actions led to the monopoly of Microsoft in every market segment it entered into, although other larger technology companies challenged Microsoft.

As he stepped down as Microsoft CEO, he continues to maintain the positions of Chairman and Chief Software Architect for Microsoft, while devoting more of his time to his own charitable Foundation. *People may change once they have reached the top - hopefully for the better. Perhaps at the top, you will tend to realize that life is not about your own success and riches or fame and intellect.* Gates also professes to "hope that *one day all people, no matter where they are born, will have the same opportunity for a healthy life."*
Gates was at the right place with the right resources to greatly influence other successful people like Warren Buffett, who has pledged to donate a great portion of his fortune to the Bill and Melinda Gates Foundation. With the accumulated riches, Gates was able to perform many

charitable acts until he received the KBE Order, which carries an "honorary" knighthood for his contribution in reducing poverty and enhancing the health of many developing countries, by Her Majesty, Queen Elizabeth II. Only British citizens can enjoy the full privileges of this order.

Back to the business environment, Gates knows very well that dissatisfied customers are the business' greatest teachers to help your corporation grow further, no matter what your company may be. Instead of working against them, he welcomes their critique and feedback. *That is the true art of manipulation in any office politicking environment where you make your foes think they are your allies.* Gates was very successful in influencing people to accept his new and different lifestyle, nearly as successful as he was when revolutionizing the computer technology industry.

Microsoft was successful because Gates was not fearful to stand for what he passionately advocates, such as his persistent position against software piracy, although his move was unprecedented and he faced much resistance. But by being persistent and passionate about the issue, with a foresight of the value in the future, Gates' efforts paid off handsomely, and established Microsoft as a most successful commercial business entity, although not without a price on his reputation for his unsavory business approaches in his business practices. He was dragged to legal courts on major antitrust actions by authorities and organizations while his company enjoyed success. He has been found to play hardball in the business environment that caused violation of U.S. laws in his business approaches. Critics were upset with Gates' monopolistic and anticompetitive practices, used to safeguard his organization. *This is also office politics at a higher level in the business arena with different businesses competing for the same market pie.*

Gates, as a young boy, would spend most of his time working on a computer to figure out the capabilities of the machine. He used his talents to develop a computer game of Tic-Tac-Toe, which the user can play against the computer. In school, he bonded well with Paul Allen over their common interest in computers, although they were of different characters. And though they shared their enthusiasm over computers, they clashed frequently over the use of the machines while developing many workable businesses and learning programs. *This is the working out of the office politics trait, 'scratching each other's back, where both great minds develop something magnificent and look out for each other until success comes.*

Computer enthusiasts were not happy with Gates as he advocated usage of software with payment to encourage developers to continue developing quality programs, to lash out against software piracy. He was known to have clashes with Micro Instrumentation and Telemetry Systems (MITS) president, Ed Roberts, over software development and the business direction as they differed in opinions and work ethics. *While climbing up the ladder of success is easy, staying at the top is quite a challenge, for there will always be contenders for the top position.*

All these are part of office politicking. Clashes will happen and one needs to stay focused and strong to persevere. There will be victors and victims in any office politicking environment.

Gates" outspoken nature made him the organization's natural spokesperson, and he would personally review every product code lines, with rewrites where necessary. He was not idle at the office or out of the office where he would promote Microsoft products aggressively.

Gates encountered some business ethics issue in a case where he was accused of withholding certain information to favor his organization. The case arose when he met up with IBM in 1980 to close a deal in developing a basic operating system for IBM's new personal computer, although he had no solution on hand. Gates later bought a similar operating system rather cheaply to sell to IBM at a much higher price while endorsing Microsoft's exclusivity on that operating system without IBM's knowledge.

Gates and his company were later sued for withholding business information, but admitted to no wrongdoing although an out of court settlement was made. *It is hard to establish good standards for business ethics that are acceptable to every player in the market. It is always a case of "one man's meat is another man's poison." Every businessman is out for himself. It is no different in the workplace. In just one setup – every employee is out for himself. Office politicking triumphs! There will be manipulations and unfair practices in the office environment unless one is alert to them.*

Staff number increased as the organization's revenue grew. When Paul Allen was diagnosed with Hodgkin's disease in 1983, he resigned from the organization, but rumors had it that Gates ousted him while others claimed that Allen preferred to use his time more wisely than on work. When Gates made his organization's shares public, they increased quickly in value to make Gates an overnight billionaire.

But Gates was never fully secure over his company's status as there were many who were against him over the years. He had to keep looking over his shoulder to identify his competition as he spurred on the fast track with a competitive spirit, which he also expected from his employees. *When one is active in office politicking, he will never be secure about his safety as it may be difficult to identify any potential backstabber. There were many who would have loved to see him or his company fall. The Bible does state: "you reap what you sow."*

Gates fits the bill in practicing office politics effortlessly due to the nature he has – intelligence and good business acumen. These enabled him to take on stereoscopic vision in business development from the product development and corporate strategy umbrellas. He is adept in corporate analysis with thorough investigations and all possible profiles of potential outcomes to any business dealing. Gates adopted a unique management style, wherein he is continually confrontational towards his employees, constantly challenging them to come up with new and ever more creative ideas. The ruthlessness that Gates was known for bringing to competition was utilized in his dealings with employees, to the extent that many were losing self-confidence in their abilities and ideas. Gates was very well known as a ruthless competitor in business where he would push forward with his company's Windows solution that is competitive to IBM's OS/2, which was developed in an attempt to bring down Microsoft. *This is a strategy of office politicking where competition must be removed as soon as possible to clear the path for your own progress.*

Gates continued to forge ahead to improve Windows by expanding its foray of functions that would be compatible with all in-house products, but not with outside software such as OS/2. This strategy killed off any competition for Windows in just two weeks and established Microsoft's monopoly of using Windows as the computer's operating system. Gates" aggressive marketing approaches brought investigative charges against him and his company for unfair marketing strategies and practices. Some allegations include Microsoft securing unfair deals in which computer manufacturers would install Windows on new computers or sell Microsoft's Internet Explorer (IE) with a Windows operating system (OS) on any computer.

Although Gates faced many challenges in his business approaches, he is very innovative in deflecting the challenges and sidetracking the pressure so that his company has survived through the challenges, seemingly unscathed, like the man himself. To Gates, nothing is formidable enough to make him lose track of what he has set his eyes and heart on as he relentlessly plowed through the challenges and difficulties, using his business acumen and personality trait to bring success as he foresaw it.

The office politicking advocator or ally will usually be frowned upon by the outsider or a business competitor, as the former is seen to be manipulative, adopting unethical practices, practicing unfairness and using his trump cards to meet his ends. But in reality, there are always some office politicking strands in the competition too. Not all is fair in love or war, not in businesses or the workplace.

d. Mahatma Gandhi

Everyone knows Mahatma Gandhi was a great "warrior" for India, who fought peacefully, without violence, inspiring many to his cause, nationally and internationally.

Gandhi was born in India during the British rule where India had been properly tutored to submit to the British instead of resenting and resisting. Indians were educated, and political subjection was reinforced through moral and intellectual servility.

Yet, Gandhi and many predecessors and contemporaries worked together in their own lifetime to pave the way for independence for India. Already in motion were the various intellectual, moral and social consciousnesses which Gandhi mobilized in a grand march with many top personalities of his time, who shared that spirit of sacrifice for India's independence. Gandhi, in his ingenuity, garnered this spirit to become an instrument of a great political-cum-moral mayhem in the nation. Gandhi was in the right place at the right time to undertake the work he had set his sight on. He appealed to the conscience of man, especially his own brethren, with a strong moral force that he lived and died for India.

He was appealing to the world with his servile attitude and acting as a friend to all - not just to a nation, race or religion.

When Gandhi died, India had gained her independence and Gandhi was honored as "the Father of the Nation" for his patriotism, politics molding and nation building. A free nation mourned his passing. The nation's "dumb millions" found their voice and recovered their rich heritage. A great battle was won without violence; this boosted the morale of the people and gained the world's admiration and attention. This miracle of a vast nation gaining its independence stemmed from Gandhi's genius architectural skill of living by faith but with no dogmatic philosophies for his followers to expound on. His path was one of honesty and relentless pursuance that brings no injury to any living thing.

Another lesson from Gandhi was that he really was no genius; he exhibited ordinariness in his early life with no mystical visions or performances. Gandhi was known to be shy, which was a handicap for him, but the passion in his spirit developed in him, an iron will coupled with moral sensibility to become what most know of him. He was indeed a self-made man, which is exemplary for all to follow.

His strength was his endurance of pain to a new height spurred by the great desire in him to fulfill the restless moral within. Gandhi was continuously striving and searching for the truth, which can and should be realized in terms of human relations instead of being abstract or metaphysical.

Gandhi moved and acted slowly but steadily, taking one step at a time; a step of action that was as capable as himself until he reached the top – his goal. He made no leaps and bounds in his quest as he journeyed on consistently. These *are similar steps that an adverse office politics advocator may also take on. He is on his own journey, to chart his own path of success, quietly and surely as he takes each step and plans each move in the office environment. He acts subtly and may be in disguise.*

Einstein complimented Gandhi on his efforts to persevere in his quest, making progress through the small steps forward, which surprised "generations to come." Gandhi showed every ordinary man that he was like them in every way but through perseverance, he achieved "success;" so can any other man. This was the inspiration Gandhi left to mankind. *Whereas Gandhi was simply guided by moral and intellectual consciences without divine portents and mysticism, the adverse office politics advocator may sideline good morals and conscience. This contrast shows that indeed there are always two sides to a coin. Some will use their good to promote good for others while others will use their good for their own benefit only.*

After much persistence on his quest to free India, he was granted political freedom with governing power, which, to the surprise of many, was rejected by Gandhi. He chose to embrace the lone pilgrimage of planting love and courage in the desert of terror and hate, trying to reconcile the Hindus and the Muslims. *Gandhi is indeed a stark contrast of the office politics norm, although he does not have any office or position. He did not grab the rewards that came with his quest, having endured much and making little progress. Gandhi did not seek fame or fortune, as most in office politics do. He was not looking to be honored or recognized publicly, which, had he been interested, public office would have presented the opportunity on a silver platter.*

Gandhi stayed focused on reconciling two hostile communities with efforts to get rid of fear and suspicion towards one another, even at the age of 77. He traveled from town to town on his quest, requesting people to make amends on their wrongs to the Muslims, while collecting alms for the homeless and injured Muslims. However, Gandhi met great resistance towards his cause as many Hindus retaliated against him, but he stood his ground. *Even without an office, when it comes to dealing with people, there is bound to be opposition.*

In the political arena, Gandhi opposed the partitioning of India to pave the way for the withdrawal of the British from India. Although India was partitioned to be free on August 15, 1947, Gandhi went to Calcutta to sooth raging communal riots and a miracle happened. The year long riot halted as Muslims and Hindus became sociable with each other while Gandhi fasted and prayed. But it was a short-lived joy as communal frenzy sparked again two weeks later.

Again, Gandhi fasted for peace to return and it did. Many who participated in the riot came to Gandhi begging for forgiveness until September 4, when all community leaders signed a pledge of peace on Calcutta. Gandhi broke fast with that achievement. *There is a lesson to be learnt here: although it may be thought that one man may not make much difference, Gandhi proved his critics wrong. So it is with office politics; the management may think that one man is "just a drop in the ocean" in the company, especially when he is at the lower rungs. But as there are rungs, there will be keen pursuit for anyone determined and ambitious enough. Never underestimate office politics!*

Gandhi encountered communal hysteria at Delhi with Hindus and Sikhs taking the law into their own hands, looting Muslim homes and seizing mosques. Innocent bystanders were stabbed. The government was helpless, even with stern measures imposed, as there was no public cooperation. In the midst of chaos and fear, Gandhi came in his loincloth bringing comfort and courage to the afflicted and frightened, while restoring sanity.

His birthday greetings from the world were met with personal sorrow that the nation was still smarting from hatred and killing. He stayed in Delhi to calm the tension, as there were some sporadic outbursts of violence even though Gandhi desired to move on to Pakistan to appease the frightened and harassed minority **Muslims. He must have experienced an overwhelming emotion of helplessness at the prospect of trying to negotiate peace between the Hindus and the Muslims. He steered the people to search inwardly for that "light." A week later, various** Delhi communities and organizations passed Gandhi a written pledge to "protect the life, property and faith of the Muslims and pledged that riots against them shall not recur in Delhi." Gandhi broke his fast while **chanting passages of scripture from many religions.** *Gandhi exhibited a religious strand, although he claimed no alliance to any particular religion That was what Gandhi stood for: the acknowledgement and devotion to a higher power than he, or else in this life, chaos and riots follow, as evidenced by India. Without a belief in God, office politics will reign chaos in our work lives and chaos in our daily lives. It is impossible to live without your Maker.*

Gandhi's fast provoked the Hindu extremists as much as it touched millions of hearts around the world, as the former felt Gandhi manipulated the Hindus in their conscience to appease the Pakistani Muslims. Gandhi was attacked the following day with a bomb thrown towards him; luckily it missed its target. But this incident did not deter Gandhi on his mission. *Although he had no office and employees, Gandhi was misunderstood by many who chose to view his actions their way. While some were supportive of him in his movement, others were doubtful and angered over the way he took matters into his own hands. Office politicking works pretty much along the same path. You may be minding your own business, but others can misconstrue your good intentions with negative labels that can be hurtful. It is hard to get away from "office politics."*

Although Gandhi prayed every evening with the crowd, no orthodox rituals were followed. People were free to express themselves in their own ways and according to their own beliefs. Gandhi just raised the topic to the intended spiritual and moral planes, appealing to the righteous way of life. Though the crowd could balloon up to hundreds of thousands, Gandhi had no protection from the Hindu fanatics who were impatient with his doctrine of peace and love. This aroused violence and hatred against the Pakistani Muslims who abused the Hindus there. Gandhi refused police protection as he continued in his struggle to sow peace and tolerance amongst the different communities. He exercised living by love where, he claimed that death is an appointment to the end of life. "To die by the hand of a brother, rather than by disease or in such other way" would give him more joy, with no hatred or anger against his assailant.

Indeed, on January 30, 1948, as Gandhi rushed to a prayer meeting where hundreds were waiting for him, a young Hindu man from Poona district forced his way through to Gandhi, firing three shots directly at his heart from a small automatic pistol. As Gandhi fell, he uttered "He Ram" – God's name[1]. He died before medical aid arrived. *In any altruist's endeavor, there will probably be more victims and martyrs than survivors and heroes, although the former may be viewed as the latter sometimes. In office politicking, there will be victims, advocators, survivors and heroes.*

Hence, Gandhi died at one of his own people's hands, although he only lived for his kind, some of whom failed to understand what he was representing for the nation.

The nation of India grieved over Gandhi's death, which impacted the nation greatly, leaving a deep legacy and living within the hearts of men, as every deed of Gandhi had been for the people. Gandhi had etched his name in the world for peacefully demanding freedom to India and Pakistan, and freeing millions of caste, tyranny and social degradation. Gandhi's death was not in vain, as it brought an end to the hysteria and violence that had been a way of life in India for so many years. His martyrdom formed the democratic character of India. It is not possible to equate Gandhi's moral influence to any material worth. His gift to humanity was great.

Gandhi is an exemplary model of approaching a problem through non-violence. This can be applied in the office where a worker can take this non-violent approach to confront any office politics. Many may rise up against you and be heated in their dissatisfaction over the way you work, but as Gandhi had it, stay true to your course with peace and tolerance to douse the flames of dissent and lack of cooperation. Your peaceful manner of solving issues and problems will impress the authorities and move others to your support or cause in due time, if you do not give up halfway. Peace and patience are excellent virtues to advocate in life and in the office environment, as they will impact others, for everyone has a conscience towards right and good.

SUCCESSFUL PROFILES – SURVIVORS OF OFFICE POLITICS

Successful Christian Businessmen

There are success stories and there are success stories. It is good to read how certain people could succeed where many have failed. What do these have that the latter could not grasp to enjoy the same success? The following profiles share a commonality: they have God as their

---

[1] Literally, "Oh, God!" Source: Wikipedia

cornerstone in their businesses. They used the Bible to direct their work ethics. They feared God and He blessed them in their businesses. They also went through challenges and rough patches at some point in their lives before they tasted success. It was never a bed of roses for those who want success, but life is more than success that the world can offer.

e. Guy Carlson

He is a successful entrepreneur who made it past the office politics by keeping to his priorities; focusing on the true issue is very important for one to succeed not only in business, but also in life. Guy was hardworking at his business but he made sure that he made time for the necessary and important issues rather than concentrating or wasting his time on things that are unproductive, like office politics. It is important to make a list of our priorities and keep to it as our beacon in our daily lives to be productive, and success will come effortlessly, as Guy testifies. With his priority list, Guy focused his energy and time on the right issues and toward the right direction, in and outside the office; to reap the good he sowed everywhere. His life was consistent in and out of the office, home and community because he was guided by the priority list he had made. Guy claims that "chasing success following conventional wisdom was elusive, as if trying to climb a greased pole" but keeping his priority list helped him stay focused with less energy used or wasted in his pursuit of success.

f. Dr. James P. Gills

A renowned ophthalmologist, Dr. James P. Gills, also experienced "office politics" during his earlier years of medical practice, where fellow ophthalmologists sneered at his methods and credibility, obviously envious of Dr. Gills" natural talent and success in his practice. Unkind remarks and accusations were hurled against Dr. Gills for not spending enough quality time with his patients as he operated on more than the usual number of cases per day. His perfected devices and procedures were deemed "outrageous" and "unsafe," but Dr. Gills held firm to his stance, being sure of himself and his procedures. Time proved him to be a true visionary in his procedures and new devices in ophthalmology. One way in which Dr. Gills handled the "office politics" graciously was to relocate his practice, knowing that the world is big enough that there are plenty of opportunities elsewhere instead of wasting his time and effort "fighting the fire." He responded to these challenges with an acknowledgement that "when you stick your head up above the crowd, somebody's going to take a swing at it." Knowing that there are challenges at most facets of life and business, Dr. Gills chose the gracious way to move on with his talents to bless others. Dr. Gills showed that although "office politics" will surface in whatever form, an individual must rise above the ordinary crowd, and continue on the journey to success.

g. John Beckett

As the president of R.W. Beckett Corporation, Beckett succeeded in his career through the use of his well-proven business principles of "integrity, excellence and a profound respect for the individual (worker)," which his corporation works on and identifies as the corporation's "core values." Beckett's approach of treating his employees with profound respect differentiates his corporation from others, as he views each employee highly instead of looking down at any of his workers, regardless of his or her situation in life or at the office. This attitude is emulated to across the board, with employees respecting one another and not allowing office politics to surface in their work environment. Because Beckett embraced a high value for every employee, they emulated the same attitude to be more productive in the organization. *Beckett understood that God is His creator and the Creator of all, so respect for all men has to be exercised and self-exaltation needs to be restrained or cast away for the common good. A fear of God is the beginning of all wisdom. (Proverbs 1:7)*

h. Zig Ziglar

Every businessman or businesswoman knows Zig Ziglar. In fact, every person who wants to be successful in business will know Zig Ziglar, the world renowned American motivational speaker and successful businessman who has written many books on succeeding in business.

Although he was from a humble background, Ziglar found the secret to success through his faith in Jesus with his own unique positive philosophy.

His real name is Hilary Hinton Ziglar and he was the tenth of twelve children who endured much hardship during their young lives with a single mother working hard to care for her children.

Ziglar pursued a sales career through selling pots and pans, improving his selling skills over the years. He developed many great sales techniques with the underlying principle "help others achieve in order to achieve what you want."

Ziglar believed that success is not only a measure for business, but also in the home. He believes that one needs to get going immediately if you want to be successful, instead of waiting for all conditions to be favorable, as success does not come overnight and it is a journey one must go on, step by step.

Having had his fair share of customer complaints, Ziglar took it all in stride. He accepted the fact that not everyone is going to be as enthusiastic about his product as he may be, and that complaints actually translate into more opportunities for repeat business.

Stress plays an important role in our work performance as well as home performance, and Ziglar experienced it too, where stress at work could affect harmony at home and stress at home can affect your work performance. Hence, a good balance to handling both sectors is required to achieve the maximum output of an individual.

Ziglar believed that it is possible to be rich towards others and feel good about it instead of exposing others' weaknesses or material riches out of envy and greed, which is really a reflection of an attitude that determines your attitude in life. How successful you will be in life is dependent on your attitude and not just your aptitude or capability.

 The need for motivation in the workplace is often a bone of contention among management and workers alike, however, **it is** a crucial and essential feature. Just as we need regular baths, regular motivation perks up an individual's performance at work or at home. Humans are intelligent beings who can receive and analyze information fed to their minds to form their character and hence, need to be wise in this ability to be what they should be. If a person has no goal for the day, he will be deemed a dreamer who is wasting his time. Therefore, we should harness our strengths toward the day's goal in order to achieve what your ability warrants. According to Ziglar, in order to achieve, one must first realize their full potential. It does not matter if it is in the workplace or in one's personal life, one must always work towards the highest level they can attain.

When you are placed in the position of managing people, your technique is determined by how they are viewed by you. If you treat them well, chances are good that they will perform in kind. Likewise, if you treat them without respect, it would not be surprising if their respect was not directed back at you. Ziglar commented that a "big shot is just a little shot who kept on shooting;" persistency pays dividends. Even when there may be persistent problems, these can be overcome with confidence as there will be some appropriate solution. Hence, our lives need a goal to set us on the right path; success and life fulfillment are not chances but choices, which one must make.

With regard to work and employees, research reveals that issues that are important to any employee are: to perform interesting and meaningful work; to be recognized for the job well done; and to be informed about the organization's happenings. All this gives a sense of belonging to that environment. Ownership and relations are important to any human being to function well in any environment.

Ziglar nearly did not fulfill his life calling as he had medical problems as an infant. He was given up by the medical profession, but was revived when his grandmother prayed over him. *That is the power of a great God who loves whom He has created. There is a purpose designed for each one that will be life changing as well as life-fulfilling. (Psalms 139:13-16).* As he went through a difficult childhood of poverty, he grew up ambitious, wanting to be successful and to make lots of money. His road to success was not smooth; he underwent his share of disappointments along with his accomplishments. The important point was that he never gave up, and he never became over-confident. He remained humble, and was grateful for every success he achieved. But when Ziglar let nature run its course, the puzzle pieces came into place and he was awarded job after job.

Ziglar went through bad career moves, too, when he was young and first started off. His initial business failure left him with an "inferiority complex" in subsequent business ventures, until he was motivated by an encouraging mentor and moved from zero to hero. As a field manager, Ziglar experienced many obstacles that tested his integrity and capability, and he struggled through them all until he found his niche as a motivational speaker, leaving his sales career. When he **realized that spiritual truths were integral to his life, he allowed them to direct him on the path of success and Zig discovered more truths acting on his life**. *When God is given charge of your life, He makes all things work for good to those who love Him (Romans 8:28).*

i. Dexter Yager

Dexter Yager today operates a multimillion dollar business after starting off in Amway in a small way in 1964. He never went to college but through hard work became one of Amway's most outstanding distributors. Although he suffered a major stroke which left him paralyzed on his right side, Dexter was determined to walk again, which he did after years of physiotherapy and great determination. He did not give up on himself through that difficult time.

He not only built up his *company* to be a 400+ employee-strong company in North Carolina, he also built up his seven children in the *corporate* world, making them proficient in *organizational* dealings. Dexter manages two Amway-related businesses with his children: Intercontinental Communication Corporation of America (ICCA) and InterNET Services. ICCA is responsible for producing audiocassettes, music tracks and videotapes while InterNET Services provides support service to Amway distributors under Yager's downline.

Dexter achieved the status of Crown Ambassador in 1985, the highest level in Amway but his vision kept increasing. The Yagers also support an African orphanage and charitable organisations.

Dexter believes that "Christians should reflect success wherever they are, especially in business." He believes that as a Christian, he should be on the giving end, not the receiving. He likens those who give generously to sponges that can absorb more than those who hold on to what they have; they will lose what they hold tightly, either through loss or decay. *He exercised 2 Corinthians 9:11 where God promises to bless those who are willing to give.* He also exercises prayer in his business as he feels that it is an important ingredient for the Christian in business.

The truth of the matter is hard work and personal hands on are very crucial for a successful business *but without God, the riches come and go easily and there is no real satisfaction on the work of your hands. One may aspire to climb the ladder of success one rung at a time as he holds on to the big dream that he has in front of him, but without God, there is loneliness and fear as you walk each step or climb each rung. Dexter experienced a lot of fears and discouragement on his way up.*

But Dexter has God in his life and acknowledged His guidance and involvement in every part of his life that he did not allow difficulties to thwart him off the path of success. He learned to put aside the small issues in life that office politics can bring on and fester if not handled correctly at the offset. Dexter exercised generosity in sharing his knowledge and skills with others, especially today in his capacity as a motivational speaker. He goes around helping people achieve their dreams just like he did but the biggest challenge he faces today is convincing people that God wants to bless them in their work or business. Dexter operates on the simple philosophy of having a dream to keep on the track of success.

SUCCESSFUL PROFILES – SURVIVORS OF OFFICE POLITICS

Bible characters

j. Adam and Eve

A couple created by God (Genesis 1:27) to enjoy life in the Garden of Eden with no worries and cares, no work, only fun and enjoyment. Yet Eve "played politics" in seeking for "advancement." She was intrigued and tempted by the serpent, who made her all sorts of false promises. The thought of being "as God" was so enticing that she allowed greed to overtake her in order to attain her desire. Her greed got the better of her and she committed herself to that wrongful path, and not only herself, but she involved her closest partner, Adam, as an ally.

Adam and Eve were shown the exit from the Garden of Eden with all their blessings stripped away as they started anew on a hard life, sweating and toiling for a living, while experiencing pain and suffering.

What foolishness we bestow upon ourselves when we allow greed to get in our way and blur our focus. The saying is quite true that "we don't appreciate something or someone until we lose them." Regret is too late for many situations. Certain events cannot be undone.

Office politics may backfire not just on an individual but also on those close to us, as all involved parties get hurt in the end. Hence, it would be wiser to think before we act. Weigh the pros and cons and be far-sighted before we launch on any office politicking paths. "A bird in the hand is better than two in the bush."

k. Cain and Abel

The first brothers born to the world were also the cause of the first bloodshed (Genesis 4). How terribly sad! Cain, the elder brother, and Abel worked at different sections or "departments" and hence, produced results that could not be compared "apple for apple" of course; but Cain did so and was upset that his results did not seem as impressive as his brother's. Cain felt discouraged and begrudged his brother's commendable efforts, nursing his grudge even though his superior reprimanded him. He changed not for the better but plotted against his brother. Setting the "trap," he led his brother to the field on the pretense of a friendly outing, but Cain attacked and killed his brother, Abel.

Anger is an emotion that one must learn to control and exercise great self-restraint before it overwhelms the individual to an unpleasant consequence. It is one of the most dangerous emotions man has to face and conquer.

If we become envious of our colleagues, we may plot and devise ill plans, which may bring negative consequences upon the self and others. Envy in the office should be wiped out, as each performs to his best capabilities, for responsibilities and expectations differ. We need not step on one another's toes while we work, and we should not need to compete by checking up on one another.

A great man once said, "When you do more than what you are paid to do, eventually you will be paid more for what you do." Maybe others do get ahead of you, but when you preserve your integrity in the office, it is bound to show and will pay off in due time. Hence, you will gain a better reputation as well as a bigger remuneration.

l. Abraham

Abraham was quite a manipulative character. Motivated by fear, he manipulated his wife to pass herself off as his sister for fear of his life in the midst of a foreign land so that he might receive good treatment on behalf of her. Although he became rich through his "favored" connections, his ruse, or *half-truth,* was finally discovered. Others around him paid a price.

His character seemed to change for the better when he dealt with his own kind – his nephew, Lot. Abraham had become very wealthy and Lot, his nephew, benefitted from his uncle's wise investments and was quite established in his own right. But their subordinates bickered and jostled for territorial power, until Abraham decided that they must part ways; he offered Lot first preference over the place of settlement. Of course, as with human nature, Lot chose the better portion. This is the basic character of man; self-centeredness. But Abraham displayed the opposite virtue – others first, self second. Perhaps he really grew wiser as he grew older. But in the end, Abraham dwelt in safety as he flourished in all his undertakings, while Lot faced many challenges in his supposedly "greener pastures."

Politicking never comes to much good at the final outcome. It is better to steer away from danger zones than to venture into them, thinking that we are strong and capable enough to withstand or overcome. Frail as we are as humans, we fall easily to the pressing situations and may need to be bailed out.

It is possible to change for the better in your character, as you live through your mistakes and let your experience refine you along the way. You will enjoy more benefits as you opt for wisdom and safety rather than quick fixes or get rich quick schemes.

m. Sarah and Hagar

Office politicking has no gender preference; it can affect man or woman. In this case, there were two women who competed for the affections of one man, gloating over one another when a small achievement was attained, which fueled the competition between them. In Genesis 16, it was noted that Hagar, a maidservant rose to equal rank with her mistress, Sarah, after producing an heir for Abraham. When elevated, Hagar forgot her humble beginnings and took on an arrogant attitude of despising her mistress. But she forgot that Sarah was still above her in status and she did hold some trump cards in her hands. She managed to oust Hagar from the household when she could no longer bear Hagar's contempt.

When one executes politicking without remembering your humble beginnings, your past will surely catch up with you. Humility is a virtue and will keep one on the right path of success instead of trying to eliminate your competition and making enemies along the way. We are never certain of the stronger "ammunition" which our opponents may have and we will be the casualty if we make foes instead of friends with our competition.

Others may bear with you for a while, especially when you are newly promoted to a higher position, but your arrogance leaves little to be desired. When the tolerance level reaches its limit, others may lash out at you when you are least prepared. Why subject yourself to such negative abuses and consequences? Don't forget your roots; they nourished the stem (character) to success. A Malay proverb aptly puts it, "*Bagai kacang lupakan kulit*" – literally translated: the nut forgets its skin cover and hence, was eaten. When we forget where we are from and stop striving to be our best through integrity, we will be consumed in this competitive and unforgiving world.

n. Laban

As recorded in Genesis 29, on the outset, Jacob and Laban seemed quite an amicable pair. They respected one another in their business dealings as well as in terms of status. But a closer look reveals a lot of political wheeling and dealing, with one trying to best the other in every situation. Laban manipulated Jacob to work for him for seven years with the promise of his younger daughter's hand in marriage, an arrangement to which Jacob agreed, as Rachel, Laban's daughter, was fair and lovely. But at the end of his service, Laban tricked Jacob into accepting his elder daughter, Leah, as his wife, giving an age-old excuse **that the elder must be married before the younger.** Jacob was convinced by Laban to enter into another seven-year agreement, or "work contract," for his beloved Rachel.

When one is not alert to the office environment, you may get shortchanged in the process. It may not be favorable to you, but there is little you can do to change the situation other than to wait for the right opportunity to come for escape or to patiently serve your time. One must be wise and discerning to the changes in the environment of work and interaction so that you can always step back and out of any precarious situation instead of falling into its trap. We do not need to participate in politicking. We would do well to be on the lookout for signs of trouble brewing on the horizon, just as one would watch for a tsunami or earthquake and flee from these affected areas before they happen.

It is seldom that one is not given notice for any bad situation. There is bound to be some sign or symptom, but you may miss it if you are not alert to the changes surfacing, no matter how subtle they may be.

o. Jacob

Jacob does not enjoy a particularly good reputation in the Bible. He was known as the "usurper" or "schemer" due to his reputation as a smooth talker and flatterer. He successfully convinced his wives to leave their father to move to another place to settle down. He was a sweet-talker, giving very plausible reasons for his actions, making himself a "victim" in the eyes of his listeners and supporters, gaining favor and strong support for his future ventures.

Genesis 31 records that he had acquired much wealth learning the trade from Laban and maneuvering methods and information to his favor. As he grew older, his priorities and loyalties changed. He had more people to feed and care for; hence, he planned and plotted against Laban until Laban's sons were quite dissatisfied with him when they realized that their fortune was shrinking as Jacob transferred their father's wealth to himself very cunningly.

When you are too presumptuous, others can climb all over you and you would not be any wiser. When you have something of worth at hand, you should always take note and take care of it, keeping it in your sight and safe possession at all times in case there are others who may snatch it out of your possession in one way or another. Once it is taken from you, it can be quite difficult to regain your lost possession. Crying over spilt milk does nothing to recover the situation. The usurper might have covered his tracks well and is already far away out of sight and contact, while we are left dazed, still trying to figure what happened.

A great proverb goes like this: "There are some people who will watch what happens while others make it happen with the rest still figuring what had happened".

p. Moses

A great leader in Biblical times who led the whole nation out of a foreign land to lay claim on a new settlement did not have a smooth journey. He had a great and supportive superior, and the distance was considered short, but the task was quite uphill with the many different types of people he had to lead and deal with. A simple journey that could have been covered in weeks took 40 years to complete! The people under Moses' charge were quite a challenge. They were full of complaints and murmurings. They were stubborn and had their own mentality, which often differed from Moses'; they challenged Moses over his authority and leadership ability. They were an impatient lot, unwilling to wait for the right timing or instruction and preferred to take matters into their own hands, making excuses and conditions.

As their leader, Moses tried his best to be humble as much as possible and appease them as best as he could, giving them their needs and desires so that they lacked for nothing. But these people kept looking back at the "good old days" when those were not really that good and favorable for themselves.

These people were complacent and were not eager or excited to look forward to their new abode. The journey was too long; no end was in sight and they were tired or bored of the same activities or lifestyle.

Moses carried out his instructions as best as he could. He also applied listening skills to the people and heard their complaints, working out solutions for them as well as accepting their suggestions, such as division of duties and delegation of authority to more of the people. Moses went the extra mile to intercede for those who wronged him and who went against "the management." He did not take them to task as they deserved and he forgave them for the wrong they did to him. Moses overlooked their faults as he nurtured and trained them, teaching them the ways they should take on, yet most of the teachings fell onto deaf ears as these people chose to do what they desired, to their own detriment.

The people's actions cost Moses dearly too, for although he did everything in his power he could for this group of people, there was one point where Moses "lost his cool." His tolerance level peaked and his patience broke when he succumbed to the people's constant grumblings against him and their superior.

Politicking can create havoc that can get out of control, no matter how capable and qualified one thinks he is. There is usually a breaking point in everyone. We should not think we are able to handle politicking alone. Sometimes we need to walk away for a while, to cool our heads and come back with a clearer and more objective mind and spirit to tackle the task, perhaps with "reinforcements" if possible.

The "crowd" in politicking may overwhelm us but it is not impossible to overcome them. As was said of Moses in the book of Deuteronomy chapter 31, verse 30, "one man can put a thousand to flight." It is the same for us when we walk with integrity with the right backing from above.

q. Samson
Many are familiar with the tragic love story of Samson and Delilah, no matter what version you may have heard; the gist is the same – a hero was betrayed by the love of his life. Love blinded Samson – literally - and caused him to be careless over his commitments. It is recorded in the book of Judges, chapter 16 that Samson poured out his heart and soul to Delilah, who used him to her advantage, knowing that he was so taken with her. She manipulated and teased him while making gains by liaising with Samson's enemies to betray him. She sold Samson's secrets to his enemies, who used them against Samson and caused his downfall which otherwise, would have made Samson the most invincible man of his time as he was renowned for his great strength and might.

Politicking in the office environment may come on in subtle ways where one may befriend another to gain some advantage for self. That is basic human nature – all for self! The enemy may be amongst you without your knowledge; it is like having a mole in the company who was sent in disguise to obtain important information on behalf of the competition.

One must not be so gullible at work that you reveal everything about yourself to others. All employees should be mature and responsible, able to work professionally and differentiate the personal issues from the work-related ones. When you are too open to anyone in the office, others may use your personal information against you, especially when they need to save their own skin. Personal affairs and love relationships are not very healthy or professional, as they are quite subject to office politics. Moreover, one can never confirm if the relationship will end well or badly. The latter would create ill feelings and might be the cause to pit one against another unless one party moves on from the organization.

One must be vigilant in the workplace; no matter how long you have worked for an organization, nor how firmly entrenched you feel, you still need to protect yourself from office politics. It is essential that you act in a mature and professional manner at all times, and insist on the same respect from your colleagues.

Be humble and do not show off unnecessarily or excessively; it may provoke others to envy and jealousy.

r. Samuel

Samuel was one of the greatest and most influential leaders of his time. He enjoyed great success in his "career" ever since he established his leadership role. His word was strong and effective. As he matured, he listened to his "boss" much more closely than he had when he was a youth. Nevertheless, a willing heart and a correct attitude helped him to distinguish right from wrong. Samuel identified to whom he was accountable, and gave his mind and heart to that focus and did not waver despite comments, gossip or actions from other people. He had very strong backing from his superior as he always acted according to his instructions precisely. He had a very open and humble relationship with his boss as he heard his tasks clearly and went about them with great diligence. His stance was very established so that no one could uproot him in any way. And after a while, no one did because all knew the upright and firm character of Samuel and that it was futile to go against him. It was better to make Samuel a friend than a foe, as many found out through the sufferings that impacted them.

Samuel's great ability to lead a big group was evident in the success he enjoyed, along with those he led, all the days of his leadership until his death. His caring heart for his people won them over as he would diligently visit the people at different places and times. He took time to understand their problems and issues and he spent time serving them, as recorded in the book of 1 Samuel, chapter 7.

Alas, the people's hearts grew cold and awry as the days went by. Instead of being content with their good life, they itched for more; they were like the "Joneses". They protested that Samuel was getting too old and was not suitable as a leader anymore. The people nearly raised a coup and Samuel stepped aside humbly as their leader as the people adamantly sought a fresh face, which was a detriment to their future.

Great things do not last forever unless they are imperishable. Your success will not last forever, nor will your favor with your superior or subordinates, if you do not constantly upgrade yourself in terms of qualifications, experience, credibility, and expand your capabilities, soft skills, character and wisdom. But the truth of the matter is, everyone ages. Dementia might set in. Our motor skills and reflexes may not be as quick and sharp as before.

One must know when to step down graciously after a time, and to leave in grace and credible standing than to be ousted in shame. A good evaluation of self is crucial to identify the current situation to check on how relevant our skills, knowledge, qualifications, advice and experience are to the situation today. It is a competitive world. Values and morals change faster than you can blink your eyes. If you are not in pace with the changes, you are considered "obsolete," a "dinosaur" or a veteran – that is, retirement is most appropriate.

All the good that you have done for another or for the company does not account for too much now. "You must be relevant;" "You must be current;" the boss screams at you. You may think "do not rock the boat if it is moving in the right directly smoothly" but your directors want more, More and MORE!

What should you do? If the pressure is too great, and the stress is beginning to take over your day to day life, it may be time to consider a change of employment. If you find it difficult to improve your performance, this is a good indicator for what action you should take. The grass may certainly be greener on the other side and it would be better for your health. Some battles are not worth fighting. Some battles are only meant to taunt, and you may want to consider keeping your integrity and reputation as you recede graciously rather than being coerced into a situation where you are unable to perform. That one lackluster performance will be remembered, rather than your other past successes. It's not worth the agony and demoralizing comments that have nothing to do with who you really are and what you stand for!

There will be someone or another organization that will appreciate you, as each has their own role to play in their own time - just like the child who grows up to be a working adult and then takes on the role of a parent before moving on to becoming a grandparent. Different people will appreciate the different roles held at different seasons of life. Then it will be a fulfilling life – satisfying and well spent! No one ever says on his dying bed, "I wish I had spent more time at the office."

Handling office politics wisely gives you further mileage not only in your career but also in your character and in your life.

s. David

David was a rare gem - one of a kind even though he was a mere shepherd boy. He minded the sheep until he was brought forth to the limelight and his life was forever changed. He did not go seeking success, wealth or fame but they came to him. He was destined to take on great things and to be a great man; he was first introduced in the book of 1Samuel, chapter 16. So, David was at the right places at the right times, even when those situations did not seem very beneficial, but David took it all in stride, sooner or later, if not during.

He remembered his humble beginnings and enjoyed great friendships, such as that with Jonathan, although circumstances caused them to part ways. David was daring and fearless, and stood firm and strong in his values, which helped him to overcome big challenges such as fighting a giant without the appropriate or expected arsenal. His battle strategy and weapons were simple and tried; something that was familiar to him. He did not try to change himself to suit his surroundings. David used his background and upbringing, which shaped his character and personality to portray himself consistently with everyone he came into contact with.
He was not pretentious until he was overcome with covetousness during his mid-life crisis. Well, goes to show that no one is perfect, even a rare gem!

David was full of energy, spontaneity and *joie de vivre* that endeared him to many, but also caused a great deal of jealousy from those around him. Some were intimidated by his good looks, others by his skills, and still more by the many favors that were bestowed upon him. David fought many battles and faced many enemies but the more dangerous foes were the ones closest to him who felt unsettled by his presence and ability; he was his own foe as well. Although he was a genuinely sincere person, David was often misunderstood. Those in power worried that he might feel that he had something to prove, and become a threat. In reality, he was a man who respected and cherished true friendships. He had a very forgiving nature and did not avenge his foes who meant him harm, for he trusted in God to avenge.

David also used his talents well, e.g. his artistic abilities in songs, poetry and dance, besides the skilful battle maneuvers and strategies. He had the boldness and leadership ability that attracted the respect of many followers and supporters even onto the battlefield. His fame spread far and wide, causing fear in the hearts of his enemies even before he reached them.

David was also very fair to his men, treating each one equally as depicted in the book of 1 Samuel, chapter 30 where the loot was shared equally amongst those who were at the frontline and those who stayed back with the supplies, due to exhaustion. He was respected as a fair leader who was not biased in the distribution of wealth, as he believed that every member played an important and necessary role in the whole process; that each was a piece in the puzzle.

It would seem that material wealth was not his main priority; some trait which many of us would do well to learn today in our materialistic world. As he gave away his wealth, he seemed to gain more!

That is the power of giving; when it is not on your priority list, you are able to use it to its optimum value without feeling shortchanged or poorer. Someone great said "he is no fool if he gives away what he cannot keep." When we can evaluate our worth in terms of talents, possessions, ability, knowledge, wisdom or character, we can identify so many ways that we can bring something of worth to another. The word of God also says, "it is more blessed to give than to receive" in the book of Acts chapter 20, verse 35. Though many do not embrace it as easily, it does not mean that it is untrue. You never know until you try it out yourself.

Every man is special and should be treated with respect. No one should be manipulated to another's benefit, but everyone should desire the best of another. As we look out for one another, our actions and values will filter out any politicking to create a healthy environment for work or living. The same principle applies in every situation.

As the saying goes, "when joy is shared, it is doubled; when sorrow is shared, it is halved." Why don't we practice this logical and beneficial proverb more often as we, mankind, are of the same kind? Don't the "birds of a feather flock together?"

It only takes one person, as David exemplified, to make a difference; and it was such a great difference – such a positive impact on others' lives. Remember the true story of the little boy on the beach, taking up one starfish at a time that had washed ashore, and throwing each back into the ocean. Is his seemingly futile action worthy of any impact when there are so many starfishes at the seashore? Yes, it does to that one that he just threw back into the sea. One person's life can be impacted greatly when you decide the right way to carry on with your life or work.
It only takes a spark to get the fire going… but think of the effect of warmth generated from the fire.

t. John

This disciple of Jesus portrays quite a different character from the rest of Jesus' disciples (there were 12 in totality). John was more a people-person, caring and always at their side, just as he was **always** found to be at Jesus' side. He valued relationships and his writings in the book of his name emphasized that aspect greatly. John related mainly Jesus' relationships with individuals as he was more that kind of character, valuing friendships and relationships. No wonder Jesus instructed him to care for his earthly mother just before he died, for Jesus knew John has a caring heart for others. John must have shown himself trustworthy to be entrusted with that privilege and heavy responsibility by Jesus.

John was not vocal but once convinced of an issue, he was a stickler, a loyalist, because it impacted him to be true and he embraced it fully without doubt, although he still did not have the boldness to step out like some of the other disciples.

John was always curious with people-related issues, such as the time when the disciples were told that Jesus had risen from the dead, John and Peter were the first two disciples to run out to the tomb where Jesus was buried to "check it" out (John chapter 20 vv 3-6). John outran Peter to the tomb but it was not his nature to take the initiative. He did not mind letting Peter take the lead.

Another time, John was curious to know what was transpiring between Jesus and Peter, just after Jesus had returned to show Himself after His death (John chapter 21 verses 20-23). He followed close behind them as they were deep in conversation. It was not John's **nature** to eavesdrop on purpose but to understand the situation fully to record the events accurately. However, being naturally gentle and soft-spoken, John was able to obtain relevant and important information even from Jesus, such as the name of Jesus' betrayer. He earned himself another feather in the cap to record future mysteries in the last book of the Bible.

Anyone can be a good tool to fuel up or douse political flames at the office. Like John, a good-natured, get-along-with-everyone personality; a people person (albeit quiet and seemingly minding his own business) can be on very good terms and standing with almost everyone in the organization. He may not be a "firefighter" at the office in any outstanding position, but he certainly will be able to douse "office fires" personally and on an individual level. He works behind the scenes and may not call for attention or credit on himself. He is the kind that will leave a legacy wherever he has been.

Gentleness and being soft-spoken are great virtues advocated in the Bible in the book of Proverbs chapter 15, verse 1 - that "a soft answer turns away anger but a harsh word stirs up wrath." Never believe the adage, "sticks and stones may break my bones, but words cannot harm me;" it is a fallacy. Words can make or break even the strongest man, for words flow into the soul of the man. Physical wounds can heal quickly but not emotional wounds; the latter tend to fester and become "cancerous" as they are harbored deep in the recesses of our souls. Hence, personalities like John's should consider it a blessing to be able to use their words wisely to dispense knowledge instead of folly, which then reflects the foolish nature of that individual. But at times, some people may misunderstand your good intentions and misread your actions without giving you the opportunity to explain and clarify, but only time will tell.

These traits are very crucial in confronting or subduing office politics as there must be the right "peacemaker" for problems in the office need to be handled carefully. Both words and actions are easily misunderstood, particularly in a volatile situation, and it is helpful if those involved do not continue to "fan the flames." So, be a "fire-douser" rather than a "fire-starter". Many will appreciate your efforts.

u. Peter

Peter was a very "colorful" character and one of Jesus' frontline disciples, always where the action was - bold and brash, but teachable. He grew to be a great leader although not without flaws even in later years. Perhaps like it is said, "old habits die hard." Peter was one of the first disciples called by Jesus – he along with his brother Andrew. He was called Simon but Jesus changed his name to Peter which means "the rock" (Matthew 14:18) to indicate the kind of strong role he would take later in his life.

Peter's life was a learning curve. There were hard times for him but with his strong and bold character, he stood up to the tests and the demands of life and responsibilities. Yes, he did waver at times and his brashness caused him to bite off more than he could chew but he would not be defeated easily. He had a non-defeatist attitude. He admitted his weaknesses and resolved to correct them along the way. Yes, Peter's life was a learning process but all these experiences built him up to be the great leader of his times.

His boldness encouraged many to emulate him, to fear nothing and no one, to go where one must go and to do what one was called to do. It is indeed a good virtue if it is executed well and not rashly. Many respected Peter and looked to him as a true leader, listening to his advice and abiding by his decisions, emulating his actions and teachings. Peter was decisive and a no-nonsense character, though some may have found it harsh at times to swallow his reprimands, as with the case where a couple gave false information and Peter knew the exact situation as well as the couple's wrong attitude. Though it may sound harsh, a death penalty was sentenced on the couple but you would need to understand the intensity of that situation during those times to appreciate the sentence. But when Peter made a decision, nobody queried; that was the strength of Peter; he commanded respect and obedience. Hence, it was up to Peter to check himself to hold true for what he stood, otherwise, a fall from grace was likely.

Today's world has a lot of Peters, too, where the personality is bold and brash, fearing no one, to bulldoze their way through thick and thin in pursuit of their values and beliefs. While it is good to have this kind of character at the office, it can also cause the waters to ripple or stir up a storm. This kind of character needs to be identified quickly by a mature leader to take him under his wings for nurturing and character building. Just as Jesus did for Peter; he needs to be guided or reprimanded where necessary, and taught to understand the overview of the situation instead of being myopic. Experience will be a good teacher too, but it may be at an expense that one may not wish to cherish as part of life's learning.

This kind of character can be like a "loose cannon," as the phrase goes, if unguarded or untamed. He really does not mean harm or malice; he just does not have the proper training or care to nurture him and show him a better way to deal with life and people. Others may feel intimidated by this kind of character or outraged and offended as feelings might be hurt, without any apology. To work well with this bold and brash character, they need to be refined, mentored and encouraged for deep down, they are quite passionate and emotional but these gentler aspects rarely surface as the boldness and brashness take precedence. A mentor is vital in a business environment. That employee has usually been with the company for a significant period of time, and can help a new employee to understand, the ethos of the company, and how to become a better overall employee and an asset to the organization.

v. Paul

Paul was actually Saul before he had his name changed to reflect a different personality and responsibility. The life of Saul (Paul) is recorded in the book of Acts in the Bible in chapters 9, 15 and 16 and from chapters 21 to 28. It makes for a good read on how office politics came his way and how he handled them.

Saul was born with "a silver spoon" in many ways. He was well educated by the best teachers of his time with regards to the law, making him very knowledgeable and above others in his intellectual standing. He was brought up with the proper etiquette, and groomed to be a great person. He was born a Roman citizen, a privilege held by very few when the Romans ruled the land, raising him above others in the social ladder. He was passionate in embracing what he was taught in his childhood days, embarking relentlessly on his one-minded mission or quest as he grew, joining and leading others to douse out the prevailing new movements that happened during his time.

It took a drastic event to stop Saul in his tracks and turn him 180 degrees. Maybe few can experience the same as Saul but when they do, it will be a life-changing incident, like those who are on the brink of death; they will never be the same. Their outlook and values have been completely "overhauled." Such was Saul's experience that he embraced a totally different mission and outlook from a certain period of his life, committing to his new path even when he faced dangers and perils all the way. He stood by his beliefs having **undergone** a dramatic personal change. From that day forward, no one was able to change Saul's mind, once it was made up. Although Saul had not expected this life-changing experience, he learned from it, and continued to live by what he discovered. No one, except God, can foresee what the future holds.

Saul was like Dr. Jekyll and Mr. Hyde in the reverse order; he was such a different character because of one significant experience in his life. Although his personality did not change, his name changed and his mission in life changed; the latter changed the path of his living and directed him all the way to the end of his life.
Paul, Saul's new name, was always working with people. He had a great influence over people, whether he was Saul or Paul. He was highly learned and was very eloquent in his presentations. He was very passionate about his cause and was highly motivated to reach the end through the thick and thin of it all. People tended to feel intimated in Saul's presence until they got to know him as Paul, for Saul was quick to "prosecute" and "persecute" those who were "wayward" from the traditions. Office politics can bring out the boldness in a person as it did with Saul; he boldly challenged those who set out on a different path and he would execute "disciplinary actions" on them.

So, it was with little wonder that people did not embrace Paul after his personal drastic life-changing experience, for his harsh dealings with some people left many in fear of him. It took Paul much effort to win others over to him later, having to prove himself over and over. That is how it is when a trust is broken in a relationship. A lot of time is spent and much effort is needed to repair that "trust bridge." He experienced much difficulty in getting into the other group after a role - reversal (as Paul), and faced the same "prosecution and persecution" from his original group which he had imposed on those who were wayward on traditions. It is a case of "tasting your own medicine."

Paul had to prove his sincerity to gain the trust of the wayward group and worked slowly to build the respect from others.

Once Paul was accepted into the new "fold," he worked hard to establish his mission by co-operating with others and not stepping on anyone's toes or claiming another's territorial gains". He set off to work on new territory so that he would be more fruitful on his mission and could continue to enjoy the support of other leaders.

Paul was a good speaker and debated very eloquently to prove his points. He challenged others to refute his claims and suggestions boldly as he was totally directed with his life focus.

With such a strong character, Paul would surely offend someone although he tried to tread as cautiously as he could wherever he worked. Once he had a bad disagreement with a fellow worker with whom he had worked so well in the past, as recorded in the book of Acts chapter 15, and they had to split up their partnership. Paul had to change team members! The cause of this disagreement stemmed from Paul's strict self-discipline on himself and others who work with him, and he could not tolerate unreliability and poor self-control at work. One might think that Paul acted harshly against his fellow workers but that was how focused Paul was towards his mission or goal. Once he received his instructions, he embraced his assigned task in totality and was quick to get on it the best he could with all the strength he could muster.

Paul needed people to support him in his work and this was reflected in various occasions when he was bound for trouble, if not for the kind assistance of his reliable co-workers who worked out a solution for him. Because Paul managed to make many inroads in his mission, he gained much support from people of like mind who were always on the lookout for his welfare. That helped him to continue with his mission amidst the hiccups.

Paul had to **introduce** himself before authorities and rulers to defend himself on the work he had to do. He was a very good **compere** and could engage many in his debates. He upheld his integrity even in tempting occasions, although it set him back in time on his mission.

Paul dealt with all levels of authority respectfully and proved himself to be a great leader in every situation. Paul found favor with many different types of people with whom he worked, although his own kind treated him with contempt. As the saying goes, "you cannot please everyone."

There are many Sauls and Pauls today. Some may even have had a 'Saul-Paul" experience. Whether you are a Saul or a Paul, your outlook on life is very simple because you will have a very clear goalpost, which could be personal or work-related. As a '"Saul", it blows your mind how others could be "doing their own thing" and not be aligned to your "goal". You might try your best to convince these oddballs to see things your way with or without much success.

If you were a 'Saul" who has turned into a "Paul", then it may need more effort on your part to work and gain respect from others whom you might have intimidated or offended.

Let time be your healing essence as you keep tirelessly and consistently at your changed attitude or character to convince others of a real change in you. As with the famed saying, "only time will tell." One needs to learn from any office politics experience.

A strong character in the work environment is frequently perceived in a negative light and is bound to ruffle a few feathers. Hence, the strong individual needs to be cautious in all his or her approaches so as not to insult anyone so as to avoid any office politicking from arising. Stay clear of difficult people as much as you can to prevent any fuselage of fireworks as the world is big enough for all. Garner support from those whom you are able to spark off well and keep them updated on your quest progress as it would auger well on you in times of trouble or difficulty.

Keep enhancing your strengths and refining your presentation skills to keep yourself marketable and up-to-date with current affairs so that you will always be ready to give a good presentation of any issue when called upon, even at the last minute. Keep focused on your goal or quest and stay close to your support group for comfort, encouragement and protection, for truly no one is an island, and no matter how strong one thinks he is, he is not infallible. It is a good idea to cultivate friendships in the workplace in order to establish a support system. If the situation ever arose where you needed assistance, it is useful to have a good support system already in place to help you through the difficult circumstances.

OFFICE POLITICS – FREE ENVIRONMENT? (8)

Is it then possible to have an office environment that is free from office politics? From the above examples, it can happen if effort and time are put in consistently, for office politics do have a way of creeping back up when our guard is let down.

a. Solutions from World Experts

As mentioned, there are many approaches to overcome office politics. Here are some listed by world experts.

1) Making a Choice
As there are many solutions to a problem, there is always more than one choice in dealing with office politics. Hence, it is YOUR choice to be involved or not. Not all employees like to be confronted or engaged in office politics, and they choose not to be involved. It is a basic human instinct to withdraw from confrontational situations depending on the personality you have. Many who try to avoid office politics understand that it is a long-term "affair" that can be very time-consuming and encompasses risks. To avoid being hurt in the process or end up in the aftermath, many **may opt** to stay away, which is a smart move. Not all can win at every office politics situation. Besides a damaged reputation, active involvement in office politicking is never healthy for your career in the long run.

Many employees miss the boat when they **prefer** to stay and fight in any office politicking entanglement. They do not realize that it takes guts to walk away from an impending danger than to confront it, just like you would run in the other direction if you see trouble brewing in front of you, especially when you gauge that the size of trouble is more than you may be able to handle.

You win at office politics when you **make a conscious effort** not to be involved in it. It pays to say "No".

2) On the Right Focus
One must always be focused on the real objective at work. You go to the office to work, not to be involved in constant conflicts with your co-workers. You were hired to perform for the company's benefit in terms of productivity to result in profits, which in turn benefits you, the worker. There is the 'service provided'/ "rewards promised" system. You work to deliver and you get paid. That is what a job is about. You were not employed to waste your time or other employees and especially the company's, on any other function that can reduce your productivity. Your strength, physically, mentally, emotionally and even spiritually, can be sucked away when you do not have the right

focus. Hence, do not get diverted by the loud booms of office politics, no matter how distracting it may be.

The company will look on you more favorably in the end when you stay focused on business objectives rather than personal ones, which is the basis of office politics. It always takes two to tango and when one party is not concentrating on the moves, the dance goes awry. So it is with office politics.

3) Circle of Influence

The workplace is frequently converted to a war zone. Therefore, it is hard not to harbor negative feelings towards your colleagues, superiors, management or even the general corporation. The demands of superiors and clients or the uncooperativeness of colleagues and subordinates can make you so frustrated that you are tempted to lash out at them in some form which can turn ugly and gives rise to office politics.

There may be many **circumstances** which you, as a middle management or lower-level employee, may have no or little control over, but negative play will not accomplish great things in the long run. Hence, it is better to keep a cool head and heart to influence the people in order to diffuse the hot **state of affairs**. Everyone has a circle of influence, or the **encouragement** of people, to empower him to perform a task in any **conditions.** You can impact others who are generally **accommodating** of you through non-violent means to diffuse the tension built up in any office politics situation, just like Gandhi (see note below). No matter how timid you think you are, you do have some **colleagues who may back you up** for the common good of the workplace.

4) Fair Play

It is a usual case to find yourself between two sides in any office political situation. This may be like the Malay proverb, "The mouse deer suffers when caught between the fighting elephants." It is a difficult position to be in as both parties could be superiors or very good colleagues of yours. Siding with one or the other will cause a bad outcome for you; therefore, it is best not to side with any party. You may be proactive by lending a listening ear instead of the hand or mouth. In this type of situation, the more you say, even if it were to appease one or the other, the more problems may arise. Words are very dangerous at these times as they are often misconstrued or communicated inaccurately. Both parties involved tend to be very sensitive in situations like this and often wrongly hear well-intentioned words. If you wish to be a peacemaker, it's better to wait for an opportune time to sit both parties down for an open and fair communication to resolve the issue. `

When you indicate your stand of not taking sides but still remain on good terms with both parties, your efforts will be appreciated and your friendship valued. Trust is built and you will have fostered a deeper and stronger work relationship with your colleagues. Otherwise, you might end up losing one or both parties' friendship.

5) Stay Professional

It is very easy to let tempers blow in an office politics situation when you are wrongly accused. It is quite natural to "give him a taste of his own medicine" or give him a piece of your mind. However, it is quite unprofessional unless you are his superior or professional counselor who is offering advice to diffuse the situation. Ticking another off will only aggravate the office politicking as the other party might misconstrue your actions, or query your authority in the situation. Although the urge is there to "teach him a lesson," it is best to avoid personal confrontations in office politicking. When you are not drawn into the battle, there can be no war.

Remember that the office is a workplace where one should be productive in their performance for the company's wellbeing; and that requires a professional attitude and behavior. It is better to garner your energy into building good working relationships than to expend it on unhealthy practices such as office politics. Professionalism wins every time at the workplace for that is the kind of worker the company really wants. It is able to see through the situation and its employees, which may not be favorable for you if you are constantly working on winning at office politics.

Involvement in office politics will cost you your good reputation as others may also play you out and make your work life difficult or miserable. The golden rule is to "do to others what you would want others to do to you" and that is always the good thing to remember.

6) Patience is a Virtue

In any negative situation where you find yourself, it is common to feel that you have been made a scapegoat or that an injustice was heaped on you inappropriately. However, there are always two sides to a coin and it is a wise move to get the whole picture first before becoming offensive or defensive. It is mentioned that "quick to hear and slow to speak" will save the day. It is recommended to hear out all parties before you form an opinion or make a judgment that is rash and unreasonable. You might end up being labeled negatively.

Most of the time, it is a communication problem between people to start a spark. People feel misunderstood and react in "self-defense" but the flames can be doused with patience. A good listening ear will work wonders. Usually we react to justify ourselves and slant towards a defensive or offensive approach, which neither benefits. The best approach is to be patient with the involved parties until all sides are heard and the whole picture is laid out for a clearer and unbiased view of the situation.

If there are some experienced and mature associates to assist in the situation, it will be of great help in resolving the conflict more quickly. It is proven that listening to understand the situation better first is very impactful in resolving conflicts at work although many do not exercise this conflict-resolving step due to the defensive or offensive nature of the involved parties. Encouraging involved parties to air their complaints for a better understanding of the situation requires lots of patience and love, but it is worth the results.

7) The Success Factor
Very often, we have been brought up to be competitive and to excel in whatever we do. Our parents and teachers may have taught us to win or be the best and to stand out above the rest with perhaps the following clause, "… at whatever means." This actually encourages conflict as you build up your personality to be domineering or aggressive, for you have heard that only the strong will survive. But it is not true. Everyone is to be respected. No one should be put down in any way, especially not for you to rise. Stepping on another to go up the ladder is not an ethical lifestyle or work style.

It is a misconception that if one is to win, another must lose, or that there can only be one winner. Life is more than winning. You cannot win at everything all the time, anyway.

As an employee, the main responsibility is to be as productive in our performance as we can be but with a fair playing ground. Others want to succeed just as much as you do. All have been employed to function for the benefit of the company. If every worker looks out for one another instead of for themselves alone, there will be enough successes to go around. Accountability towards your own responsibility will encourage success to come your way.

Success is for everyone who puts in the required performance appropriately. If everyone plays his part, there can be no office politics. No one needs to lose if each understands the simple law of "together we stand, divided we fall." Employees in conflict can hurt a company and bring it to its downfall.

b. Management's Role

There are many ways to keep office politics in its place, even if it can't be totally avoided. The management can do the following:

a) Ensure Buy-In

Everyone in the office must want to get rid of office politics, starting from the very top of the echelon to the lowest rank. Every employee and employer must share the same vision and value of creating an "office politics"-free atmosphere as their preferred work environment. This can come in the form of a motto, a company vision statement or slogan that can be clearly conveyed not just during orientation but also in annual team—building or conferences. Every person must embrace this stance of company ethics willingly; that should build up loyalty and responsibility. This stance should be reiterated regularly as a reminder to the employees, as man is very forgetful or can slant off easily. Reminders will keep the employees on their toes as well as keep them focused while being like-minded to foster better relationships with one another.

b) Encourage Open Discussions

There must be an avenue for all workers to voice their opinions and dissatisfactions on any work- or office-related issue that is not provocative or threatening in any way towards them. No bias should be formed nor should any negative action be taken - directly or indirectly - on those who provide the feedback. It should be construed as constructive criticism for the betterment of the organization. Although this important task is usually reserved for the Human Resources or Personnel Department's portfolio, the proper training for relevant and trustworthy personnel is crucial to ensure its success. No biased opinion or judgments from these empathetic counselors should proceed outside the four walls of the counseling room, keeping the confidentiality and trust of the one giving feedback or opinion.

No reward or verbal acknowledgement should even be given in order to prevent employees from misunderstanding the true aspect and nature of such feedback. Positive acknowledgment will convey a wrong message to the employees that the company looks up to these more favorably than to those who do not receive feedback. And negative acknowledgement will seem like an indirect "slap on the hand" for any involved party in the situation; this, in turn, will discourage further feedback from the same person or another.

c) Properly Trained Personnel

Hence, the personnel who are counselors need to be well qualified, and not only in academic qualifications and experience. They must be people of integrity with a pleasant character, and with maturity that will draw the employees to open up effortlessly, winning their confidence and trust. This should be a group of trained personnel who are trustworthy and responsible with a 100% commitment to the company's motto, acting like a SWAT team minus the aggression. They are responsible for motivating the workers to higher productivity while being alert to keep politics out of the office environment. They are likened to the "ghost-busters" or more appropriately, office politics"-busters?

This group is like the **office** guards patrolling the workplace against **office** politics and not directing any ill manners to any person, but rather keeping the **work** environment clean and free of **office** politics. These counselors need to be trained and retrained to uphold their integrity pledges to the employees, employers and the organization overall. Training and retraining should come from outside sources or professional experts in the area of personnel and ethical work environment and should provide unbiased teaching and learning methodologies to equip these counselors appropriately.

d) Appropriate Training for all employees & employers

Employees as well as employers/superiors should undergo training and retraining on identifying and understanding office politics, the negative consequences to self and organization productivity as well as to character and reputation, staying alert and reporting occurrences of office politics in the work environment. If this training is ongoing, office politics will be kept out of the organization to allow more time for exhibiting higher productivity and revenue for the workers and organization as a whole.

Employers/superiors should have their own training sessions to be equipped with tools and methods of recognizing and dealing with office politics. Although there may be a special team in the organization that is available to resolve office politics, the managers and leaders are usually at the frontline with their workers to detect the first signs of office politics. If these are nipped in the bud, the possibility of office politics taking root and sprouting will be nil.

While the higher echelon of employees may have their own training sessions, they should also be trained with their workers or team members to create and foster a better relationship as well as to establish the same understanding of the issue. Miscommunication is very common in the workplace; it diverts effort and reduces productivity that can cause office politics to surface. Being trained together allows all levels of employees to embrace the same vision and understanding of the issue at hand, so that minds thinking alike will enhance not only a higher productivity for the organization but also will create a healthier work environment.

e) Employee-Employer Interaction

Create events that encourage employers/superiors to interact easily with the employees so that a better understanding can arise between both parties, besides narrowing the status gap. As both levels interact with one another in non-threatening environments like team-building or problem-solving issues workshops, these parties can better understand each other and work together as they share a common viewpoint or objective. They learn to complement one another instead of working against each other, fostering a healthy and more productive work environment while creating a mutual respect for one another.

Learning happens indirectly either way as each member's creativity is displayed in the various role-plays or hypothetical situations created. These are healthy activities that foster good relations amongst the organization's important assets – the employees. Office politics will be reduced to ground level as all employees at all levels gain trust and exhibit respect for one another while healthily competing for higher productivity for self and company.

c. Employee's Role

Besides the above approaches by the organization – the individual can play a proactive role in reducing, eliminating or avoiding office politics too. The individual employee can do many things in the office to create a good and healthy work environment for himself and others. Some of the ways that will eliminate office politics are:

1) Offer your hand or assistance to another colleague whom you see struggling with a task, especially if you have the knowledge and expertise. Take the initiative to offer your assistance to the colleague to win him or her over, giving you another friend at work, and thus, pushing aside any possible office politics from arising in the future. This kind offer of assistance is also very effective in developing a good relationship as well as enhancing a current work relationship, which can benefit both parties. As the adage goes, "One good turn deserves another;" the grateful colleague will be more willing to return your kindness in the future.

2) As no man is an island, it is quite impossible and unhealthy to be working all alone in an office environment, for there are definitely times where you will need the help of another, or to interact with others in the office. By staying at the sidelines, or distancing yourself from the others, you will bring more negative impact on yourself than good. Although your intentions may be good, misunderstanding is rife when communication is lacking. Hence, it is not only for your own good to maintain a good reputation, but it is also healthier for the organization on the whole, if you can make yourself aware or alert to the grapevine, without adding salt to the wound. Rumors flowing through the office are usually not pleasant or complimentary; and if it is not on you, it provides juicy news to others; such is the nature of man.

There may have been some slip-ups in security in the office environment and some crucial management news may have been leaked. It is to your benefit to be in the know and prepare yourself for any eventual situations, especially unfavorable ones in the future.

If the gossip is about the personal life of other colleagues, it is best to stay out of the loop and not add on to the circulation, no matter how juicy the piece of news may be, as the negative impact might come back to haunt you, should you add on your opinion or advice unwittingly.

You have to learn to filter out what you hear from the grapevine, retaining that which is relevant to you and throwing out that which is unrelated to your productivity or character.

3) Be prepared to stand up to your integrity should it be questioned. Others may want to test whether you are an easy pushover or uphold your integrity by spreading unkind comments or rumors against you. If there is no truth to the allegations and you are aware of their existence, you should put your case forward in a professional manner, with your facts ready to counter all the allegations one by one, if necessary, to refute any baseless claims which are meant to discredit you. When you take this upright stance, you will not project yourself as a pushover by anyone, and you will stand up to your integrity.

If the situation involves a superior, it does not mean that you are retaliating, but that you desire to confront the wrongly presented facts and wish to make the correction for the sake of safeguarding your integrity, character and reputation. This professional approach will stop the office politics from spreading like wildfire, as it is well known that "silence implies consent." At times, it is not right to stay quiet when it might discredit you; at times, you may need to keep cool and stay quiet until the right opportunity presents itself for entering into your defense.

You will need to be wise about the timing of action, whether for defense or offense, without further provocation on any party and without physical violence or aggression.

Where possible, you should approach your superior quickly with the allegations, which concern you and help him/her understand your concern about the allegations as well as clarify the true situation. Your superior will be a good and strong support for you against outside attacks on you, if you have been maintaining good relations with him or her all the while.

4) The more allies, the stronger your defense. You will need to secure the support of other colleagues and superiors before going into a counterattack in office politicking. If you have been upright and true in your character, then it is easy to garner the support in your favor as your allies will vouch on your integrity of character and back you up on the issue. Although time and effort are expended in this exercise, sometimes, it is necessary to take this step to quench the office politics once and for all. A one-time inconvenience will take you on a lifetime smooth journey while working in the same environment.

Sometimes, it is necessary to face your foe with the necessary backup artillery, although you may not come to fire them, as the amount of support behind you might discourage the attacker.

5) Make time to spend with your colleagues, or superiors. Lunchtime is a good time of interaction and establishing a good rapport between self and co-workers, or with the higher management level if the occasion arises. You need not be beer pals but it pays to go on some excursions or family holidays with your colleagues to better understand and appreciate one another outside the office. These informal gatherings provide the best platform to display the easy side of you which may incline others to see you as likeable, rather than labeling you as aloof, proud, loner, too private, or socially impenetrable.

6) It is human nature to like those who like us; and you might need to take the initiative or make the first move in showing your genuine interest in your colleagues or bosses, in a non-threatening or non-sexual manner - more of a friend or human being worthy of their respect.

7) Though one may not be able to win all the others all the time, it may suffice to win most people most of the time, as long as you don't make enemies at the other times. Whenever you can, seek out the commonalities that may exist between you and other colleagues. This is usually a very useful way to break any ice, especially if you are new to the office environment. It is also a good initiative to foster good relations between you and your colleagues, which will give others a better perception of you. Your ideas and thoughts will be better received than if you were aloof and minding your business most of the time.

8) When you do not make yourself sociable with your colleagues, they will gauge your character according to their perception and understanding, which may not be true and worse, inaccurate. This inaccuracy about you may cause an undefined tension or negativity between you and others because you have not taken the initiative to "introduce" yourself or let your colleagues, subordinates and superiors get to know you – the real you.

9) When you do not seek common grounds for a good relationship at work, you may be labeled as 'snobbish" or condescending, which may backlash at you in terms of uncooperativeness or lack of support from your colleagues.

Hence, it is advisable not to offend any co-worker in your organization but to find time to get to know your colleagues, and let them get to know you. This can be easily achieved by looking for common areas of interests which may not be office-related issues such as hobbies, values, likes and dislikes which can serve as small talk in that few minutes of break, or in the elevator or restroom.

As you attempt to open up to others, they will also open up to you and there will not be negative vibes about you as you are accepted into their fold.

10) Speaking up for self or sharing your thoughts and ideas are necessary to enable other co-workers and superiors to understand your values, mentality, maturity and even character.

But when you do propose an idea or something new, change is usually met with resistance until the defense mechanism is lowered. Hence, it is recommended to put forward new ideas or solutions which may cause changes to the office environment gradually, giving enough time and notice for others to mull over your suggestions or recommendations. Different people react differently, and changes are not easily accepted especially when others feel that all's well and there is no need to "rock the boat" when the machinery is well oiled at the moment. It is a humanistic trait to resist change.

You can start sounding off your new ideas and suggestions to a smaller crowd or just to your lunch partner, before widening your potential audience to garner support and acceptance. This approach will gain others" respect of you and they may even speak favorably of you than otherwise.

Choosing the right words and analogies when making a stance or presentation of some issue is crucial to obtaining a favorable response from the crowd or audience. The timing of your presentation is also another crucial factor to ensure a positive support than negative, as timing is everything.

At times you may have to hold your tongue, grin and bear it until a more opportune time to state your case with the proper facts on the issue to gain more mileage than to insist on direct confrontation at that moment. Patience is a virtue and tolerance is its partner. Be prepared to give your account clearly and precisely so that the case is concise for a quick grasp of the matter.

When you can put yourself forward in all issues, you will be a force to reckon with; halting all possibilities of office politicking, as it will be well known that you know what you are talking about when you speak.

11) Self-confidence is paramount to face office politics should it come upon you; if you continue to hold up your head and work with integrity, treating every colleague with respect and fairness, you will be confident of yourself and your performance. When you make time to touch base with your colleagues and superiors, there is no rivalry or competition between you and them, which puts you in high stead, inspiring respect and halting any form of office politicking.

RELATING PERSONALITY TRAIT TO OFFICE POLITICS (9)

Perhaps you might want to consider understanding yourself better before you want to jump onto the bandwagon of office politics, as others may read you better than you yourself.

There have been many studies on the types of personality which one is inclined to, which molds one's character and influences the way a person thinks, feels, does and speaks. Temperament influences everything about a person, and if you can identify yours, you can maximize your own potential as well as be able to understand why and how others behave the way they do. It would be so much easier to identify the hypocrite or the gossiper and others who are active in office politics.

There are basically 4 types of temperament: the sanguine, the choleric, the melancholy and the phlegmatic; and they are as different as night and day! These different dispositions affect everything routine about us, from driving skills, to eating habits, to communication, to family life and even to handwriting styles. These personalities can help one to understand how people with different or similar temperaments can be in conflict or clique so well together.

Understanding each person's nature will help you understand why and how different people react to office politics.

Hippocrates first suggested the characteristics of the 4 temperaments around 420 BC. He believed that each temperament originated from a different part of the body, and could assist in better understanding how the human personality functioned.

    a. The Sanguine

    A person who is a sanguine or who has this characteristic is rather warm and lively. He is probably a likeable person most of the time as he is very receptive towards others. A sanguine tends to act based on his feelings rather than logical thoughts. He is a festive or cheerful personality who tends to be considered a high extrovert. Wherever he is, the sanguine has the capacity to enjoy himself thoroughly at that moment, drawing others into his cheerful net effortlessly. He lacks no friends, as he is the live wire at any party or function. Everyone feels very much for the sanguine person who makes each person in his focus as extraordinary and special. He has the knack for making himself special to everyone he meets.

    The Biblical character, Peter, one of Jesus" 12 disciples is considered a sanguine. He is always the 'spokesman" and the attention-grabber with his actions or words spoken out there and then through his feelings rather than through careful thought.

    The sanguine gets away with many faults through his eloquence and his easy manner towards people, whom he makes them feel comfortable with him and there is no fault with him. His friendly disposition and plentiful words belie his low self-confidence but they do get the sanguine over rough patches in his life.

Being an optimist, the sanguine sees life quite positively as he lives in the present, forgets the past and is not concerned about the future. He is inspired easily to kick-start new projects no matter what the outcome of his previous project was. He views everything anew giving the same type of enthusiasm, which he had displayed on earlier projects. The sanguine tends to see the positive side of the situation and goes about working on that in that direction.

The sanguine is very sincere as he is optimistic but others, who do not quite get the quick change of emotions exhibited by the sanguine personality, may misunderstand this characteristic. Others are doubtful about the sincerity of the sanguine as he changed his moods but that is the beauty of the sanguine; he can switch moods to relate to others easily for he really cares for those around him. This special ability is God-given that he can care for others in changing himself for others as he puts them first.

Hence, in office politicking, the sanguine may come on disseminating information very light-heartedly which people may join in the cajoling with little serious thoughts to the conveyed pieces of information. The sanguine would have an eloquent way of communicating any juicy grapevine, which captivates its audience. It is quite impossible not to hear what the sanguine is saying on any office issue. It is such light information that it seems harmless, and the information seems relevant and intriguing at the moment.

Weaknesses Of The Sanguine

Anyone would think that a lively personality like the sanguine would excel in his life, which could be true if he keeps a cap on his weaknesses; and one of these is poor self-control. The sanguine may be jovial and a people-person character but he often lacks restraint in his endeavors. Hence, he can start a task but not finish it. He faces many temptations rising from his lack of self-discipline and may go wayward from his intended path as he becomes disorganized in his ways. He often gets away from his errors by talking his way out as he is very good with words and handling people. The sanguine may bend the truth to suit his own needs as he believes that "the end justifies the means." Peter, the disciple of Jesus appears to be the sanguine type of person as he was hasty and quite impulsive at times, promising not to desert Jesus but yet not able to accomplish it.

Hence, at work, a sanguine personality who is not mature is a great danger. He mingles well with others who embrace him into their circle easily with his fluent speeches but in return, may be betrayed by the sanguine if things go awry and he needs a quick "getaway" solution. A web of deception is possible by the sanguine, as he has no qualms in "slightly" deviating from the truth for better presentation. Office politicking will be in the form of exaggerated facts or distorted truths that the sanguine may present to the ever-keen and listening ears of others around. Whether the truth or not, the sanguine person's presentation is always enticing to hear and thus, the 'seed" is sowed.

One must really be mature to watch out and be on guard against the sanguine in order that you will not fall into his web of deception and be entangled unnecessarily to your own detriment. It is better to avoid interaction with the sanguine who is immature than to have bad seeds sown into self, which brings on corruption, doubt, insecurity and other negative emotions that are crippling.

b. The Choleric

The person who has a choleric temperament is usually a very practical and strong-willed personality who is quite self-sufficient and independent. He is quite decisive and even opinionated, making decisions quickly for himself and on behalf of others. The choleric is an extrovert who likes activities but is not stimulated by the environment. Conversely, he stimulates the environment around him with his ideas, goals, plans and ambitions, which he freely shares aloud. With a practical and keen mind, the choleric does not like to waste time getting involved in fruitless activities; hence, he will target on worthy tasks that will make good use of his energy and talents. He can be bad-tempered or irritable.

He is firm in his opinion and is not easily swayed by what others think once he has made up his own mind and stand on any issue. This may cause the choleric some unfavorable misunderstandings about his personality, although this personality drives him to crusade against social injustice at times as he is unafraid of adversity; instead, they fuel his passion to be standing for what he believes to be right and just. His undeterred determination leads him to frequent success as he stands by firmly with what he believes to be right. He is restrained and focused as he is very determined and confident of himself. The choleric embarks on a project with a single-mindedness that is commendable which often heaps success upon him.

The choleric is not an idle person; he works happily being engaged in some worthy activity with a keen mind on good organization although details are not his forte.

The choleric exhibits strong leadership skills and responds readily to a leadership position although his forcefulness tends to dominate others and he might be misunderstood. However, he is a good judge of people to determine their sincerity or reliability in a work environment. Once the choleric is very sure and focused on his work or direction, there is no holding him back; whether he has followers or supporters is not important to him, for he will get through the task alone. He is that sure-minded and full of self-confidence that there is no stopping him, come what may.

Nevertheless, the choleric is also a very practical person who works his way through any task he has set his mind on. Adversity fuels his passion than otherwise.

A choleric person's weakness is his emotions; he is so independent that he cannot empathize easily with others, much less sympathize or show compassion. He is not one for tears or emotional outbursts, which makes him insensitive to others' emotional needs.

The choleric is considered an opportunist in many cases where he plunges into a focused task without considering those in his path, perhaps shoving them out slightly, guided by his intuitive push. With a focused goal, he sets himself on a course, which makes him seemingly bossy or domineering; he may even recruit people, directly or indirectly, to accomplish his goals.

If the choleric can control his dominance so that he does not seem condescending on others, he will receive good responses towards his leadership.

In office politicking, the choleric would be a powerful force to reckon with. Once he is steadfastly focused on a goal, he may just bulldoze his way through from the start to the finish, regardless of whom he may knock over along the way. It is best to move out of his way when he is on the "warpath."

The Weakness Of Choleric
The main weakness of the choleric is his adverse temper. He succumbs to easy outbursts and manipulates others through that characteristic, which causes fear to those who stand in his way. The volatile choleric may spew verbal acid without hesitation arising from his adverse characteristic. His sarcasm can be quite cutting, denting the weak or insecure. To mature, the choleric needs to control his tongue and his temper. The choleric is an extremely unemotional character who does not like emotional displays by others. His lack of love tends to make him insensitive to the emotions of others around him. He quickly sizes up matters without detailed analysis, which may prove unsound at times but it will be difficult to change his mind once he

has made his decision. He can be quite crafty, manipulating his ways on others to get what he wants; he will not take "no" for an answer. When the choleric indulges in his weaknesses instead of controlling or changing them, he becomes very dominating. Moses, in the Bible tends to be choleric as he killed the Egyptian guard out of sheer hot temperedness.

Hence, you will be able to identify the choleric as he will boom loudly, making himself heard whether it is for your attention or otherwise. It is dangerous to have a strong choleric in the work place who will manipulate others to have his own way for this is how office politics surface; most of the time, you are caught off guard as you are manipulated into some devious or bad scheme without being aware of it. Hence, one must be extra vigilant in interacting with the choleric and stay at arm's length to avoid being drawn into his web of lies and manipulation. The choleric may be condescending and intimidating if one is not strong in his values and character to withstand the heat from the choleric.

c. The Melancholy

The person with a melancholy nature is very analytical and gifted. He possesses great emotional sensitivity with a good taste in the fine arts. His emotions sway him in various moods, which may at times make him out to be an introvert. It is not easy for the melancholy to make friends as he dislikes making the first move in any communication or interactive situations. He is not a relationship person unless others take the initiative to approach him. But once you have established a steady relationship with the melancholy, he will be a stalwart for you as his conscientiousness and perfectionism do not permit him to forsake his friends. He does not shirk from his responsibilities towards others who are in the pack with him, although his reserved personality tends to have him misunderstood by others as unfriendly. In reality, however, the melancholy person finds it difficult to be expressive or to open up to others although he wants to be liked.

Disappointing experiences can cause the melancholy to draw slightly away from people. However, he has great analytical ability, which helps him excel in planning tasks. The melancholy is capable of great ideas and designs for he would have thought through the idea and design before implementation to ensure its success. He is considered a genius who excels in fine arts and life cultural values. As such, a melancholy tends to harbor perfectionist traits, demanding high standards of performance and meticulous work. The melancholy is very quick in analysis and can size up the problem or project faster than another, giving the details or envisaging the related potential difficulties.

The melancholy may be very talented but he is no showoff. He is quite happy to perform his task quietly on his own capability and time to produce the best possible results. He is very self-disciplined and may expect others working with him to be the same. The melancholy tends to go all the way to give the best results; sometimes at the expense of neglecting his own needs. Hence, he is usually very tired out after a big project as he has sidelined himself in favor of the project.

The best offering from a melancholy is personal sacrifice, which tends more towards caring for others than for self. If the melancholy is able to stay focused on his strengths and not give in to his weaknesses, such as the negative mood swings, he will attain consistent success; otherwise, the depressive melancholy may just give it all up. This temperament requires firm control to keep guiding it to the right path so that it can stay on the straight and successful way.

The melancholy does not perform well at office politics. He is not very good at handling stressful and demanding pressures that come with office politics. He would probably be affected quite negatively by all the office politics and revert to depressive moods and recoil into his own hermit shelter. The melancholy is probably the last person in the office who kick-starts any office politics as well as jumps in on the bandwagon of protest. He would be quite happy being left on his own to perform his work without the stings of office politics, which can adversely affect his personality and productivity.

The Weakness Of Melancholy

The melancholy is a perfectionist; and as such, he tends to view people, things and situations quite negatively or pessimistically. He will bring up all possible negative aspects of a task before it can get going. The melancholy is also quite a critic. He is quite difficult to please because of his perfectionist nature. He assumes a high standard that others find hard to attain; even for himself. As a result, the melancholy tends to lack self-esteem. This self-centeredness causes the melancholy to be sensitive and touchy which can be unhealthily suppressed until it boils over and explodes. The melancholy is subject to mood swings, which make him very unpredictable. He will become impatient with others as he can be uncompromising and unreasonable. It is difficult for the melancholy to work in teams as he feels the lack of standard employed by others. He may have ideas that are too unrealistic to be practical. Joseph would be an example of melancholy and voicing that one day his family members would bow down to him and as a result offending his siblings.

In the office, you can identify the melancholy personality who often works alone and exhibits high standards on himself and others. His characteristics will display a lack of tolerance towards others not in sync with himself. He may put others into a bad light with his critique. One must be careful and wise to sift through all that the melancholy says; otherwise, there will be more fuel added to the fire in any office politics. The melancholy may be a one-man critic but his input can fuel the fire in the office if he is not aware of his potential adverse contribution to the office environment.

d. The Phlegmatic

The person with a phlegmatic disposition is calm and easy-going with a very high boiling point; it would be quite impossible to see the phlegmatic in any fiery disposition. He is most likeable as he views life very contentedly by avoiding unnecessary excitement. It is as if he just wants to let life pass by and he is merely doing his time, which he wants to do without any fanfare. Being quiet and calm are the vital assets of the phlegmatic. They think and plan carefully before taking the leap or plunge.

He would trade confrontation with negotiation as he is eloquently skilled to douse any anger or resentment with his cool and calming words. He does seem to fare better as a peacemaker as he does not advocate violence as a solution to any problem.

The phlegmatic is very dependable which makes him such an acceptable friend to all he meets. He will fulfill all his obligations and promises without second reminders as he works out the most practical solutions that will use the least amount of effort. That is exceptional as he works well under pressure. He can excel as a leader but seldom clamor for that position on his own; nevertheless, if he were placed in an authoritative position, he would be able to put people together cohesively for a great result.

Despite being cool and timid, the phlegmatic is very capable in other ways. He puts on a less emotional front and lacks no friends as he can put the crowd at ease or in stitches with his dry humor. The phlegmatic has a very positive approach towards life with an excellent memory although the phlegmatic prefers a non-inclusive lifestyle that does not permeate his routine living. However, his emotional strengths do put him in the forefront of standing against injustice when necessary although he may approach the situation differently from others. The phlegmatic would rally others to the same cause he supports, and would do a good job at that. However, the phlegmatic may not necessarily reveal his true self, which may be difficult for others to get to know him well. The phlegmatic does not like to lead voluntarily, although he can exhibit some good leadership traits with his strengths.

The phlegmatic approach to office politics differs from the other temperaments; he would try to be evasive wherever possible, unless the situation is forced upon him to act. He can rally support easily to his cause and would be able to move in on any unfavorable office politicking, although with great reluctance.

Dr. Henry Brandt, a renowned psychologist, in relation to the attitude on a person's strengths and weaknesses, defines maturity as "one who is sufficiently objective about himself to know both his strengths and weaknesses and has created a planned program for overcoming his weaknesses."

It is not common for most people to be able to see or understand the worth of Dr. Brandt's quotation; perhaps until later in life when one tends to question the meaning of life. In their prime, most people are busy making big bucks in any way they can without considering the consequences and impact on their character.

Understanding your own strengths and weaknesses has two major benefits: (1) you will mature as a person, and (2) you will capitalize on your strengths and improve on your weaknesses to make you an even more effective person. Hence, one should be courageous to view and evaluate one's strengths and weaknesses in the correct light so that one can mature. A mature person confronts office politics professionally, always coming out a winner!

The Weakness Of Phlegmatic

The weakness of the phlegmatic tends to be his sluggishness, or lack of drive or ambition. He also lacks initiative on a task and performs the bare essentials. If possible, the phlegmatic will generate excuses to get out of the task at hand. Nevertheless, the phlegmatic is quite sensitive and selfish, but covers these up quite flawlessly. He is also very stubborn but no one would ever think so of the phlegmatic, as he carries himself diplomatically. He can proceed through life graciously without confrontation but standing vehemently against active participation. The phlegmatic attitude is most exasperating at times when work is to be performed but this personality will graciously smile and nod, but walk away doing his own thing. John, the apostle of Jesus would tend to be phlegmatic, as he prefers to play low key.

The root of the matter is an underlying fear that grips the phlegmatic. The fear prevents the phlegmatic from venturing into the unknown and fulfilling his potential.

The phlegmatic would be the one least involved in any office politicking, as he is unmotivated or fearful. Hence, he would be quite a 'safe" character to eliminate as the source of office politics. He is a fence sitter, watching both sides with a smile on his face, agreeable to both parties but non-committal to either.

Temperaments – Not so straightforward

It is difficult to label one as sanguine, choleric, melancholy or phlegmatic as these qualites do not operate individually. It is more the norm to have a combination of these four temperaments in any person, thus making life harder to identify and to work with an individual. One really has to be a psychologist or personality guru to read a personality correctly.

From these major four elements, one can find 12 blends of personalities and there may be more with any combination of these four major components. Hence, it really takes time to study and understand the temperaments which an individual may take on.

These traits play a major role in any individual, especially through social interactions and in the work place. Understanding your own temperament(s) is helpful to point you to the right path of character development as you desire to reduce or work on your weaknesses; it also helps you to know how to interact with others and enjoy a better life as well as find the most suitable vocation; and hopefully avoid the office politics.

Vocational Options through Temperament

Every individual is born to work; unless he was born with a silver spoon in his mouth or with some physiological or mental setback. Work is a process where productivity is generated with pride and joy, especially where good work ethics are exercised. Work enriches self and brings fulfillment to not just the individual, but others around it. So, when an individual can be at a place of work that is favorable to him or her, it is considered "a dream job." You love your work; you love what you do and what you are contributing. But not all individuals are blessed to be working their dream job; for some, work is a matter of survival when it is scarce or too many mouths to feed or even when there are too many commitments to fulfill.

But if every individual can adapt his behavior with the proper work ethics at the work place, a lot of unnecessary office politics can be eliminated. Vocational frustration comes about when the individual does not recognize the best job that fits his character or how his persona can affect his productivity at the work place.

1) Vocational aptitudes for the sanguine
   With the strength of cheerfulness and liveliness, a sanguine is best suited for positions that require a lot of social interactions, such as sales and marketing. Their natural charisma attracts people to them like bees to honey where people will be most mesmerized by their speech and enthusiasm. The sanguine will be most fitted for vocations, which require their bubbling enthusiasm, which are very encouraging and catchy. A sanguine loves people interaction and enjoys motivating people he meets with his cheery smile and "life-is-good" attitude.

Sanguine personalities do not like paperwork. They prefer to be out in the field mingling with the crowd or client rather than keeping record of their activities for a report. But with some self-discipline, the sanguine can overcome this minor dislike. A sanguine needs to remember that any job comes with some aspects that are not desirable or favorable to them but work well for others, which they need to conform to keep the harmony and productivity of the organization.

The sanguine is usually a starter rather than a finisher on a job. They prefer quick success, if not instant. They dislike getting their hands dirty and taking too long on the job, which may run up against opposition or frustration.

*Hence, at the **workplace, the sanguine personality is optimal when out in the field, interacting** with the customers rather than being bored and unhappy with the paperwork at the office. Frustration creeps up and may cause office politicking by the sanguine who may find it difficult to keep his mouth shut. Since it is his boisterous nature to speak, it is better to have the sanguine out of the office where he can be more productive for the company than stir the hornet's nest.*

2) Vocational aptitudes for the choleric
   The choleric personality's activeness and practicality makes him very suitable for a job that needs hands-on involvement; he is very adept in planning and doing with a good head for a supervisory role. Middle-level management will best suit the choleric who likes to get his hands dirty, but without too much analysis and details of the job. Having a total overview of the project may not be his cup of tea. Having a developing and active nature, the choleric will be found working on tasks and projects quite happily and independently. The choleric prefers to be involved in the job than to delegate but he is capable of handling more than one job at a time even though he is not favorable to details. Hence, it is better for a choleric to have a good assistant who can take the details and analysis off him to allow the choleric to be inspired and plan.

Quantity is important to the choleric rather than quality. The choleric would make a good supervisor as he is able to motivate his subordinates with his self-confidence and goal-consciousness to ensure that the projects under his charge get completed, although they may not be performed exceptionally well . But because the choleric is such an independent worker, he may not be able to train his subordinates well or monitor their work performance better. His thinking is that praises and compliments will make his subordinates complacent in their work and thus, will lower productivity.

The choleric personalities will excel in jobs that require practicality such as teaching and building things; perhaps being in the sports or service industry like restaurants. With strong determination and self-confidence, the choleric can also excel in the army and in politics. Any industry that requires hard workers with a great deal of activity will be suitable to the choleric.

Hence, to keep the choleric out of office politics, provide him the job that requires a lot of activity that will occupy the time, concentration and efforts of the choleric that will not leave him free to be involved in office politics. As the saying goes, "An idle mind is the devil's workshop."

3) Vocational aptitudes for the melancholy
As the melancholy is quite a perfectionist, any job that requires detailed work to be completed meticulously will be suitable. Vocations that involve humanitarian aspects are the cup of tea for the melancholy, who loves to attend to people or assist them through his keen mind for in-depth analysis, sharp eye for details and a compassionate heart towards others.

Hence, the melancholy will be suited to jobs or vocations that provide service to people such as doctors, writers, actors, composers, musicians, mechanics, engineers and the like.

Although he is very gifted and smart, the melancholy tends to work with his heart more than his mind.

To get the melancholy out of office politics, it is good to set him at his own corner with his workload that he is passionate about so that he can pour out his heart and mind on the task at hand than to bother with office politics; for if office gripes get to him, he may be easily affected emotionally and may be drawn into a more introverted mode.

4) Vocational aptitudes for the phlegmatic
The phlegmatic is very patient, even with routine activities. His gentle nature encourages others to rise to the task or occasion. He creates the ideal atmosphere for learning or working, and hence would make a good boss. Most administrators, counselors and department heads are usually the phlegmatic. The phlegmatic is attracted to planning and computation, which would make them ideal engineers, statisticians, carpenters, electricians, repairmen and draftsmen.
The phlegmatic is very diplomatic and would bring order instead of chaos at the workplace. He is well organized and always prepared, punctual and works well under

pressure. The phlegmatic is usually loyal to the company he works for without thinking of moving on.

However, the phlegmatic does not like to volunteer for leadership positions although he is capable and has such aspirations. But this may not augur well for the phlegmatic personality who waits to be called upon, as many times, opportunities do not offer themselves to the phlegmatic unless he seizes the day. Hence, it is possible that the phlegmatic does not get to live up to his full potential in life. Employers may appreciate the phlegmatic but may not envision him as a leader due to his lack of boldness in being a "go-getter."

The phlegmatic prefers the 'slow and steady" type of vocation with pension and retirement in his mind; hence, civil services or secured vocations like government services may be most suitable for him. The phlegmatic is not one who would venture out to be an entrepreneur although he is most capable, but his preference for a simple life holds him back. The phlegmatic works best in building others up and hence works well as a teacher, trainer, counselor, coach, advisor, or supervisor who can motivate his wards or subordinates to fulfill their full potential.

The phlegmatic would not be the one who would be involved in office politics as it is not his nature to be at the forefront of these kinds of vibes. He is content with a simple life and has no desire to play office politics. Let the phlegmatic work where he works best – motivating others to do their best. He could be in the Human Resources or Training departments to build up others in their work productivity. Perhaps he could be a most useful instrument in dousing office politics as a counselor if such a department is available in the organization.

Working the different temperaments to enhance productivity at the workplace

As one would know, there are so many different types of people at a workplace. It is the CEO's nightmare to get all his employees working harmoniously together for optimum productivity and for the wellbeing of the organization. Hence, he hires managers and Human Resource personnel in this most challenging task. It can be said that it is a "divide and conquer" strategy that the top man employs to get good work done. The organization can be likened to an orchestra, which needs to be playing in tune to produce beautiful music. It is the responsibility of department heads and supervisors to manage their department personnel to have each give his best to blend his strengths with others for a peak performance as a group.

To achieve this productivity, it is crucial to analyze each subordinate's personality to identify his style of operation and to put each one to his best fit – like a round peg to a round hole and a square peg to a square hole – for maximum productivity.

Hence, understanding and remembering that the business community is primarily concerned about the financial health of the company, it would function to commit to practicality, cost effectiveness in its operations, and lastly personnel development to enhance productivity for a higher financial status for the company.

The company will augur better if it takes time to evaluate its employees from top to bottom, and the personality traits of each employee, and fit them into their right place at work for higher productivity (self and company) and eliminate office politicking. Not only will the office place be a better working environment, but there will be happier employees and believe it or not, the world will be a happier place too!

CONCLUSION (10)

a. WHAT ARE WORK ETHICS?

Work ethics can be simply defined as some belief exercised at the workplace by an employee in the realm of moral values of work. Work ethics are very important at the workplace; office politics thrive or deteriorate depending on the work ethics engaged. Work is where an individual spends one third of his life. It covers not just the feelings of the employee towards his job or his responsibilities at his place of work, it also involves the career path of the employee, which could go up, down or remain stagnant. Work ethics carve out the vocational path of the employee to be either the same (hopefully on an upward trend) or be totally different.

Hence, work ethics encompass behavior, attitude, ambition, interaction and communication aspects of an employee towards his job and colleagues, whether peers, superiors or subordinates, and even associates. Work ethics can reveal the "who" and "how" of a person as he goes about his work at the workplace. The true character of a person can be revealed through the way he deals with others or situations at work, even if it takes time.

There are many aspects of work ethics that involve humanistic characteristics, such as integrity and accountability. Here lies the bottom line of who your colleague really is. Although he may be sitting next to you or have been working in the same department as you for many years, what would he do when the going gets tough?

At times it is very difficult for all, even two persons, at work - to determine, much less agree, on the right or proper work ethics to take on. Even more difficult is the agreement to define improper, underhanded, grey lines, unethical or blatantly wrong work ethics.

Work ethics are not just the concern of individuals at work although they are the main players; it involves the company as a whole, reflecting on what the company vision or mission is and the way it operates; the employees catch on very quickly in order to carve out the work ethics at their workplace. The role of the company is essential and crucial to set the tone for the right work ethics to be engaged in. However, many instances have proven that shady or negative work ethics practiced, that differ from the actual vision or mission of the company, cause a lot of office politicking, leaving the company an unfulfilling place to be and a bad experience for some. When the organization does not hold up to its vision and mission statement in practice, or if it does not prioritize work ethics but profits, there will be employees who will seize the opportunity to have a field day on office politics. Manipulations of the system and abuse of authority to further their own agenda will constitute the call of the day. Office politics thrive well in these situations with this kind of employee, which can be quite detrimental to the organization as a whole if it is not checked or corrected. It will be like a wild fire spreading from one bad practice to another through the employees, which will be hard to control when it gets out of hand.

Employees get the wrong message from the management that it is all right to take any means to achieve the end. Short-term profits can be reaped but long-term profits usually elude.

Work ethics are crucial to the organization's well being, as the organization consists of people who are supposedly the greatest assets of the company and not just a building or name. Virtues like honesty and integrity, truth, ownership, good accountability and responsibility, good performance, loyalty, commitment, belonging, sense of purpose, appreciation of job or talents and unity are all very crucial and essential in the healthy growth of an organization.

It should be, even if in philosophy, that an employee should exercise the best work ethics he can, at his workplace in order to keep a clear conscience. Most people do practice good work ethics, for all have a conscience. However, there are usually a few rascals and as the saying goes, it only takes "one bad apple to spoil the whole bunch."

People should be doing the right thing at the right time in the right place. That will avoid any office politicking. But work ethics seem to be an intrinsic value in life. It is not tangible or physical to the extent that one would easily be reminded of its presence or worth. The desire to be engaged in work ethics must arise from within a person, but many are still unclear how the conscience works to be fully concerned about it. The conscience can be swept aside many a time when greed or desperation takes over. No one is really sure how the conscience works and how work ethics interweave with the conscience for a profound effect. Even the psychologists and psychiatrists are still searching for answers to the questions of conscience and work ethics today. Many questions but no real answers yet.

The world offers many possible solutions or explanations on these two areas: conscience and work ethics, but only the Creator of conscience knows the true answer. The Christian viewpoint is the one based on what his Creator has taught him. Just as his Creator God creates the human, he is shaped with a conscience to know good and evil. God instituted work ethics when He made Adam, the first man, to work for his living. Through hard work, man will enjoy the fruit of his labor (Genesis 3:19).

God created man in His own image to exercise good work ethics, to enjoy his labor as well as to be a good testimony to others, making life simple and harmonious. Hence, the proper work ethics should underpin two aspects: self humility and the good of others. Humility means servitude; that is, putting others first before self. Now, *that* is a tall order for many people. The crux of the matter is treating others as well as you would want yourself to be treated. Actually that is the "golden rule" of the Bible (Matthew 7:12) "Do to others as what you would want others to do to you." When you treat others with decency and respect, these virtues come back to you; no wonder the earth is round. That calls for treating others with respect, valuing them, believing in the good in them and encouraging them to excel. That will surely wipe office politics from the workplace.

This reminds me of a good analogy that I read before. The scenario goes like this: In heaven a large and wide table was set with plenty of good food that would satisfy any appetite. Problem was that the table was so big and wide that it was impossible to reach the food. Instead of hands, people have long scoops and hence, it was impossible to bring the food back to feed self, although one can scoop the food easily. So, one can go hungry for it was difficult to turn the food on each person's scoop to put into his own mouth. People were crying in desperation. Suddenly a bright spark suggested. "Encircle the table; scoop the food which another opposite the table likes and feed him. Then let him do the same for you." When the people did that with their long scoops, everyone had their fill for they all enjoyed the foods they like, scooped and fed by another opposite them.

Life should be like that; each of us should scoop what others like and feed them while they return the deed. Office politics would be unheard of then.

b. Work Ethics Models

One must be careful in picking the thoughts and ideas of another when it comes to building the self. Although a model seems reasonable and workable, the underlying philosophy may not be quite right. For example, Joseph Fletcher's model of work ethics, called "Situational Ethics," says that the ends justify the means as long as love is the basis of your action. This gives one many a field day to do as they please as long as they claim they did it out of love, like child abuse, when a parent punishes a child too severely "out of love." An action could be well meaning but it is still wrong when other areas are violated.

Another model is "Moral Ethics" that can guide a person in his behavior, speech and attitude. But sadly, today moral ethics are either denounced or viewed as relative. Relativity here refers to culture, circumstance and individual. It is now a world of "all depends on…" in almost everything we do or think. Right can be considered wrong if it is not convenient to the hearer, or it is a wrong considered as right if the user prefers a "think out-of-the-box" approach, which is seen as "cool" and "in" for this point in time. Hence, the foundations of our culture and society are crumbling fast under our feet, as right and wrong have been blurred.

Many are adopting moral relativism, which says morals, or ethics depends on every individual, and no two individuals are the same. Hence, there is no final standard of good or evil, as it is dependent on each person's viewpoint. But one should realize that moral relativity is actually an excuse for actions that differ from the traditional moral ethics that have existed since the world began. Moral relativists do not believe in absolute right or wrong, and judge no one for any action performed. However, one should note that there are existing laws that are considered standards for the wider public, which are set for the general safety of all. Otherwise, there would be chaos in the world with everyone standing firm on his own opinion, and there would not be work done. In reality, moral relativists are trying to avoid unfavorable peer consequences. It would be a case of "getting away with murder" literally or figuratively.

c. Defining Morality for Office Politics

Therefore, it is essential to stand by the system that has been in effect for centuries, even since the beginning of time. Morality refers to concepts of behavioral standard, conscience, identity, virtues and principles. It is getting more and more difficult to apply moral standards, as people choose to take on what they want for themselves rather than conform to the existing standards. But one must consider the importance of these guiding principles for survival, whether it refers to doctrinal issues or basic living. Fair play and harmony are needed to mold good people for a good society; hence, humans need a belief system that shapes their moral behavior. This will affect the way they work and how office politics will be viewed and handled.

Whether one accepts it or not, everyone has a conscience that guides his or her choice of actions and thoughts. Although most reasonable people accept the moral standards set for society, there are some who push forward with their own stance. These tend to take on the philosophy, "it is all right as long as I don't hurt anyone else though I may be hurting myself" without realizing that they *do* hurt others along the way and not all is right. So, it is crucial to exercise the right philosophy at the work place if high performance and rewards are desired; that will certainly cut out any office politicking. And this is precisely the reason for companies to indulge in vision and mission statements to guide their company's growth for success.

Guided by religious commitment

Another important concept of morality is the religious commitment of a person. Religious people have a fear of their god and would refrain from acts of deceit and evil although they may not be saints. But it can be noted correctly that God-fearing people already have a moral standard imposed on them through their religious beliefs, which they readily embrace, or else you are left with your own view or moral standards. Thus, many would claim morality to be a human invention, designed to bring order to an otherwise chaotic society. There is always a choice factor and sometimes, the choice made can be in conflict with others' choices. But when one refers to his or her religious beliefs, there is already a set order that guides the believer's choice and it is usually for the welfare of self and society. That will prove to be a major breakthrough for office politics.

Guidance through Conscience

Even if one does not have a religious commitment, there is still the question of conscience, which pricks when wrong or unfavorable choices are made. Conscience is a useful tool in directing our actions whether we claim to know what is right or wrong. The conscience bears witness to our actions and gives peace or anxiety to our decision. The conscience works by prompting us on our actions based on previously learned behavior or experience.

Work Etiquette

In conclusion, one should have some befitting principles to guide the self at the work place. A religious commitment with good principles is not a bad option, as the believer fears his God and is restrained from performing malicious acts, even at the workplace. A believer strives to be pleasing to his god and is constantly reminded of his role and responsibility for his existence; and that includes the necessity in doing good to others and to himself.

At the workplace, proper etiquette should be appropriately exercised to ensure that the workplace flourishes with joy and motivation to succeed without competing with one another within but rather to compete with the outside forces – the company's competitors, so that jobs are secure. Words of encouragement and empathy should be practiced extensively so that an environment where harmony and productivity can thrive. Only then can office politics stay out of the workplace for the good of all within.

d. A Biblical approach in handling office politics with "Be Happy Attitudes"

Perhaps one can consider the eight attitudes listed below to make a good change towards the workplace.

Karl Menninger states: "attitudes are more important than facts". Though many think otherwise, and hence strive for it, material wealth does not bring true happiness. Everyone is bound to have challenges in life if they are normal. With the misconception, many employees pursue wealth and fame at the workplace through office politicking but it does have a rebound effect. Many experienced people will tell you that wealth does not give you everlasting happiness. Fame is fleeting and sometimes deceptive, relationships can be disappointing and drugs are totally bad things to be avoided at all cost, if you truly value your life.

What is needed is a change in our attitude or our outlook on life to counter office politics, besides the many challenges we face in life. Robert Schuller claims that "nobody is financially secure all the time; the more you have, the more you tend to lose." Man tends to go searching for solutions in the wrong places, most of the time.

The first attitude is to seek assistance to fill the poverty we have in our lives. Poverty "pockets" exist in our lives, which we need to identify and overcome. When we fill the poverty pockets, we shall be at peace with others, and ourselves, and office politicking will be far from our minds. Poverty pockets include financial poverty, occupational poverty, intellectual, emotional and spiritual poverty, as these aspects make up a person – body, mind, soul and spirit. When you can identify what you lack, you can go about working to fill it or achieve it. Just like an alcoholic who refuses to acknowledge his drinking problem, sees no problem in his life with alcohol; hence, he would not be concerned about solving his drinking issue. Until he faces the fact that he has a drinking problem, a poverty of the soul, he continues to drink and subject his body to deterioration.

When you realize your lack, it is best to seek out assistance humbly instead of resorting to devious and cunning means, which can backfire and cause you your reputation. Success comes when you realize your poverty and seek out assistance to fill it. Intellectual poverty is the lack of knowledge, and one should seek assistance in obtaining the required knowledge which would benefit, such as at the workplace where the employee requests the appropriate training to equip him for the work assigned. Emotional poverty refers to a lack of love that one feels and as a result, tends to slant towards depression, low self-esteem and rejection of self and others. Spiritual poverty is when you lack faith or belief in God, who is the Creator of man and all. There will be a void that only He can fill. Nothing and no one else can fill this spiritual poverty but God, for He is your creator. He knows you well to know what you need. Robert Schuller writes "when your life is in a mess, stress can lead to real success, if we confess our spiritual poverty." But success is not the material success that one might have in mind. It may refer to the peace and acceptance of self and others, which is more previous than material wealth. When you have some kind of poverty and don't seek help to fill it, then others will seem uncaring but they may be in ignorance since you did not voice your need.

The second attitude is to bounce back when you face failures, instead of wallowing in self-pity or revenge. A wise saying goes like this, "the good news when you have bad news is that the bad news will turn to good news when you change your attitude." The proper and correct perspective to any situation is very crucial. Challenging circumstances can draw the courage within that you might have never known until you go through difficult times. Not looking at what you have lost, but looking at what you have left will help you be more thankful for there are many more out there who have less, than you. You may have been badly affected by office politics, but if the issue has been resolved or is past, you should move on for a better future than to hold on to grudges and revenge. The latter kills your spirit and soul.

The third attitude is to be meek – M for mighty, E for being emotionally stable, E for Educable and K for kind; not so much as being a doormat in the midst of injustice. In the core of office politics, one must be meek to face the situation. Meekness here is staying calm and having a cool head so that you are able to think through the adverse situation calmly and logically for the best solution without being irrational or unwise in decisions and action, which can lead to backlash. Hence, being meek in adverse circumstances is being strong. It is an inner strength or might that one can only unearth from within during adverse circumstances. When you are emotionally stable, you can keep negative impulses at bay; that is a definite sign of maturity in a worker preferred by any organization. Emotional instability drains physical, financial and moral resources, which only fuel office politics. When the emotions are not kept in control, you can fall easily into depression or discouragement. Educable means teachable; not that you are immature or lack knowledge but it is a sign of wisdom that one is not perfect and knows all, that there is always room for improvement and learning. The educable or teachable are not proud or defensive. If their way is not the best as yet, they will change for the better; hence, they will succeed.

Nowadays, it is rare to meet a kind soul, yet it is a good trait, which many want to adopt and display. Many are self-centered as the world continues to lure its citizens to its worldly possessions like materialism and fame. But kindness stops the mighty from being ruthless. Kindness stops the emotional coldness and hardness. Kindness checks the educable from arrogance.

The fourth attitude to counter office politics is thirst and hunger for the right things in life – they do not include wealth, fame and beauty. These will fade and cause you to yearn for more, for they never truly satisfy - unlike a true purpose or meaning to your life. Understand why you are where you are today and where should you be heading tomorrow. Each one is endowed with talents that can only satisfy the soul when used properly. Hence, in the office, when you misuse your talents, you create office politics, which can cause problems to others and self. But when you use your talents wisely, you will benefit yourself, colleagues and company. The spillover effect will be the outsiders who receive the results of your well-used talents.

It is important to do the right thing in your life, whether it is physical, like living a well-balanced lifestyle, or spiritual, where you embrace the good attitudes towards your Creator, others and self. It is easy to forget that when one thirsts and hungers for something good, he will go seeking for it. Then he will find it and be satisfied. One must adopt the "gopher" attitude – "go-for-it!"

The fifth attitude to take on in your course of work is to remember that the world is round. There is a backlash – good or bad. If I want others to treat me right, I must treat others right first. That is the golden rule of human interaction. If all were to practice it, the world would indeed be an ideal place to live, for joy and peace would rule the day. Each of us learns, at some time in our lives, that life is not always fair. But the sooner we accept that fact, the sooner we grow in wisdom and maturity. There are always two choices in life: to be happy or to be unhappy; the positive or the negative attitude. The sooner one realizes that a negative attitude causes a negative impact on our lives, the better for it is true that a negative perspective of your life can trigger health issues such as high blood pressure, stroke, stress, cancer and certain mental disorders. But when you select the positive attitude, you will view people and circumstances very differently. You have the strength to overcome adverse circumstances without letting them affect you negatively. That is a true sign of maturity.

If you look at life, you will realize that it comprises different generations. Hence, like the round earth, whatever you do can have an impact on the next generation. Just like the call to save Mother Earth from global warming, and protect the earth with recycling, man should follow suit in his attitude for the sake of the next generation. A poor or good attitude will be taken on by the next generation, as the young ones imitate the older generation's attitudes and behavior. The poem by Dorothy Law Nolte says it all, "children learn by what they live." People catch on from one another, the good and the bad. As proven in science, "For every action there is a reaction." Many have said, "life is a boomerang;" whatever good you give out, it will come back to you. If you give out bad, the bad will come back to you too. What do you want to give out today in your life? At work? How do we wish to impact our colleagues or subordinates at work? We tend to be critical of people more than we compliment them. But it is the good attitude that wins half the battle, especially when it comes to office politics. When you compliment your colleagues, you are building their self-esteem and they will be more cooperative with you. Less office politicking will happen. If you want people to be nice to you, you will have to be nice to them even if you have to take the initiative. We have read about Mother Teresa in her selfless quest to love the unlovable in Calcutta and she exemplified this attitude without thought of reward or return.

The sixth attitude is regarding the future. Everyone must die someday. No one has found the fountain of life to live forever, although Christians have everlasting life in Jesus, the Son of God who died on the Cross for their sins and rose again to live in heaven reigning with God. The question is, are you concerned where you will go after you die? Many people believe that their final destination is either heaven or hell; whether they care which one they end up in is another concern. But if there is really heaven and hell, you will certainly go to either. Which one will you choose? Hence, your preferred choice will determine your sixth attitude – living your life with accountability. Many religions believe good works will lead them to heaven or to be reincarnated to a better life form. The truth of the matter is, people want good lives or to leave a legacy when they die. How about you? Are you any different? Are you living well enough to meet your Maker at the end of your life? The Bible mentions that each one is held accountable to God when he meets his Maker. Can you think of a reasonable excuse to give to your Maker for your involvement in office politics during your lifetime?

The seventh attitude is to be fair and just. There are already many injustices happening in the world; some in our own lives. But there must be those who care enough to stop the injustice. As the saying goes, "the ball is in your court." What are you going to do about it? There are many breaches in life. Let each one do what he or she can. Remember the story of the little boy who stuck his finger in the dyke because it was leaking? He did his part and waited patiently until help came along because a little leak can cause great damage slowly but surely. So the same is true in office politics; a little grudge or murmur now and then, here and there, can build up distrust and tension amongst the colleagues, between workers and management to the extent where the whole office crumbles in value and production. Hence, you can act fairly and justly to put down office politics instead of putting others down at the work place. Fellow workers are of value and should be respected, not politicking in the office. You can be a great example to others in the office and earn respect.

The eighth attitude is perseverance. In everything, there is a need to be persevering. The famous phrases, "Only time will tell" and "time will heal" are excellent words of encouragement for one undergoing trials and difficulties to carry on his life. The office is one place that is subjected to trying situations easily with the myriad of personalities, and hence, a very good place where one's perseverance will be tested. There may be peer pressures, hurtful words, false friendships, competitiveness and betrayals with lots of drama but perseverance in your good principles will knock out office politics to your favor in due time, though at the moment, the going may be tough but again the saying goes, "the tough get going" – perseverance.

e. Finally – YOU can Make a Difference

You may think that you are like a drop in the ocean but it is precisely the drops that form the great powerful ocean. Isn't it wonderful to be part of something great and powerful? That should be sufficient motivation for you to make changes happen. It always starts with you – the single person. One can make a difference because one can impact another and another, while the other impacts another and the growth will be exponential. You can stop office politics if you want to; and others will follow suit. *You can make a difference at the workplace.*

www.ingramcontent.com/pod-product-compliance
Lightning Source LLC
Chambersburg PA
CBHW071218200326
41519CB00018B/5581